Clear**Revise**

OCR GCSE
Computer Science J277

Illustrated revision and practice

Published by
PG Online Limited
The Old Coach House
35 Main Road
Tolpuddle
Dorset
DT2 7EW
United Kingdom

sales@pgonline.co.uk
www.clearrevise.com
www.pgonline.co.uk
2020

PG ONLINE

PREFACE

Absolute clarity! That's the aim.

This is everything you need to ace your exam and beam with pride. Each topic is laid out in a beautifully illustrated format that is clear, approachable and as concise and simple as possible.

Each section of the specification is clearly indicated to help you cross-reference your revision. The checklist on the contents pages will help you keep track of what you have already worked through and what's left before the big day.

We have included worked examination-style questions with answers for almost every topic. This helps you understand where marks are coming from and to see the theory at work for yourself in an examination situation. There is also a set of exam-style questions at the end of each section for you to practise writing answers for. You can check your answers against those given at the end of the book.

A free pack of over 30 Python solutions to accompany each of the programs listed in the book are available to download from www.clearrevise.com.

LEVELS OF LEARNING

Based on the degree to which you are able to truly understand a new topic, we recommend that you work in stages. Start by reading a short explanation of something, then try and recall what you've just read. This has limited effect if you stop there but it aids the next stage. Question everything. Write down your own summary and then complete and mark a related exam-style question. Cover up the answers if necessary, but learn from them once you've seen them. Lastly, teach someone else. Explain the topic in a way that they can understand. Have a go at the different practice questions – they offer an insight into how and where marks are awarded.

ACKNOWLEDGMENTS

The questions in the ClearRevise textbook are the sole responsibility of the authors and have neither been provided nor approved by the examination board.

Every effort has been made to trace and acknowledge ownership of copyright. The publishers will be happy to make any future amendments with copyright owners that it has not been possible to contact. The publisher would like to thank the following companies and individuals who granted permission for the use of their images in this textbook.

Design and artwork: Jessica Webb / PG Online Ltd
Photographic images: © Shutterstock

First edition 2020. 10 9 8 7 6 5 4
A catalogue entry for this book is available from the British Library
ISBN: 978-1-910523-23-0
Copyright © PG Online 2020
All rights reserved

THE SCIENCE OF REVISION

Illustrations and words

Research has shown that revising with words and pictures doubles the quality of responses by students.[1] This is known as 'dual-coding' because it provides two ways of fetching the information from our brain. The improvement in responses is particularly apparent in students when asked to apply their knowledge to different problems. Recall, application and judgement are all specifically and carefully assessed in public examination questions.

Retrieval of information

Retrieval practice encourages students to come up with answers to questions.[2] The closer the question is to one you might see in a real examination, the better. Also, the closer the environment in which a student revises is to the 'examination environment', the better. Students who had a test 2–7 days away did 30% better using retrieval practice than students who simply read, or repeatedly reread material. Students who were expected to teach the content to someone else after their revision period did better still.[3] What was found to be most interesting in other studies is that students using retrieval methods and testing for revision were also more resilient to the introduction of stress.[4]

Ebbinghaus' forgetting curve and spaced learning

Ebbinghaus' 140-year-old study examined the rate in which we forget things over time. The findings still hold true. However, the act of forgetting things and relearning them is what cements things into the brain.[5] Spacing out revision is more effective than cramming – we know that, but students should also know that the space between revisiting material should vary depending on how far away the examination is. A cyclical approach is required. An examination 12 months away necessitates revisiting covered material about once a month. A test in 30 days should have topics revisited every 3 days – intervals of roughly a tenth of the time available.[6]

Summary

Students: the more tests and past questions you do, in an environment as close to examination conditions as possible, the better you are likely to perform on the day. If you prefer to listen to music while you revise, tunes without lyrics will be far less detrimental to your memory and retention. Silence is most effective.[5] If you choose to study with friends, choose carefully – effort is contagious.[7]

1.	Mayer, R. E., & Anderson, R. B. (1991). Animations need narrations: An experimental test of dual-coding hypothesis. *Journal of Education Psychology*, (83)4, 484–490.

2.	Roediger III, H. L., & Karpicke, J.D. (2006). Test-enhanced learning: Taking memory tests improves long-term retention. *Psychological Science*, 17(3), 249–255.

3.	Nestojko, J., Bui, D., Kornell, N. & Bjork, E. (2014). Expecting to teach enhances learning and organisation of knowledge in free recall of text passages. *Memory and Cognition*, 42(7), 1038–1048.

4.	Smith, A. M., Floerke, V. A., & Thomas, A. K. (2016) Retrieval practice protects memory against acute stress. *Science*, 354(6315), 1046–1048.

5.	Perham, N., & Currie, H. (2014). Does listening to preferred music improve comprehension performance? *Applied Cognitive Psychology*, 28(2), 279–284.

6.	Cepeda, N. J., Vul, E., Rohrer, D., Wixted, J. T. & Pashler, H. (2008). Spacing effects in learning a temporal ridgeline of optimal retention. *Psychological Science*, 19(11), 1095–1102.

7.	Busch, B. & Watson, E. (2019), *The Science of Learning*, 1st ed. Routledge.

CONTENTS AND CHECKLIST

Section 4

☑

Section 5

☑

Section 6

☑

Section 7

☑

Section 8

☑

Section 9

Section 10

MARK ALLOCATIONS

Green mark allocations[1] on answers to in-text questions throughout this guide help to indicate where marks are gained within the answers. A bracketed '1' e.g.[1] = one valid point worthy of a mark. In longer answer questions, a mark is given based on the whole response. In these answers, a tick mark[v] indicates that a valid point has been made. There are often many more points to make than there are marks available so you have more opportunity to max out your answers than you may think.

TOPICS FOR PAPER 1
Computer systems (J277/01)

Information about Paper 1

Written paper: 1 hour and 30 minutes
50% of total GCSE
80 marks

It is a non-calculator paper.

All questions are mandatory.

It consists of multiple-choice questions, short response questions and extended response questions.

ARCHITECTURE OF THE CPU

All computers have a CPU, memory, one or more input devices and output devices.

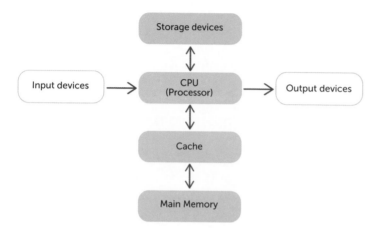

Identify **two** input devices and **one** output device that may be connected to the CPU. [3]

Input devices include a keyboard[1], mouse[1], scanner[1], digital camera[1], microphone[1] and web cam[1]. Output devices include a monitor[1], printer[1] and speaker[1].

The purpose of the CPU

The purpose of the **Central Processing Unit (CPU)** is to execute instructions stored in memory by repeatedly carrying out the **fetch-execute cycle**. The CPU contains the **Arithmetic Logic Unit (ALU)**, the **Control Unit** and several general-purpose and special-purpose registers.

The fetch-execute cycle

Every CPU instruction is **fetched** from memory. Once fetched, it is **decoded** by the Control Unit to find out what to do with it. Then the instruction is executed. Every operation carried out within the fetch-execute cycle is regulated by a 'tick' or cycle of the CPU clock.

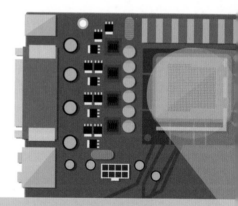

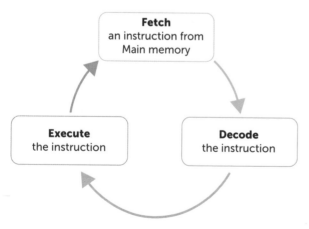

A single core 4.5GHz processor has 4,500,000,000 clock cycles or 'ticks' a second. This is known as the clock speed.

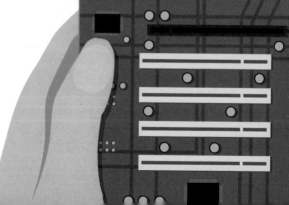

COMMON CPU COMPONENTS AND THEIR FUNCTION

CPU Component	Typical size	Function
ALU (Arithmetic Logic Unit)		Carries out mathematical and logical operations including AND, OR and NOT, and binary shifts
CU (Control Unit)		Coordinates all of the CPU's actions in the fetch-decode-execute cycle
Cache	Up to 32 MB	Sends and receives control signals to and from other devices within the computer
Registers	32 bits or 64 bits	Even smaller and faster than cache memory, registers are memory locations within the CPU to temporarily store memory addresses, instructions or data

Von Neumann architecture

John von Neumann developed the **stored program computer**. In a von Neumann computer, both programs and the data they use are stored in memory.

Identify **two** events that happen during the fetch-decode-execute cycle. [2]

The address of the next instruction to be executed is held in the PC.[1] The CPU fetches the instruction and data from memory[1] and stores them in its registers[1]. The PC is incremented[1]. The Control Unit decodes the instruction[1] and the instruction is executed[1].

MDR holds data or a program instruction when it is fetched from memory or data that is waiting to be written to memory

The **accumulator** is a register in which results of operations carried out in the **ALU** are stored

PC is a register which holds the **memory address** of the next instruction to be processed.

MAR holds the address (location in memory) of the current instruction or piece of data to be fetched or stored

CPU

Memory Data Register

Accumulator

Arithmetic Logic Unit

Program Counter

Main Memory

Control Unit

Current Instruction Register

Memory Address Register

CPU PERFORMANCE

Clock speed

The **clock speed** determines the number of **fetch-execute cycles** per second.
Every action taking place in the CPU takes place on a tick of the clock, or clock cycle. Each cycle is one **hertz** so a 3.7 GHz processor will cycle at 3.7 billion times per second.

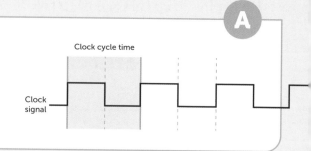

A

Clock cycle time

Clock signal

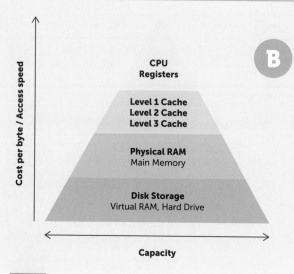

Cost per byte / Access speed

CPU Registers

Level 1 Cache
Level 2 Cache
Level 3 Cache

Physical RAM
Main Memory

Disk Storage
Virtual RAM, Hard Drive

Capacity

B

Cache size

Since **cache memory** operates much faster than main memory, data is transferred in and out of cache memory more quickly, which makes the CPU more efficient as less time is spent waiting for data to be transferred. There are two or three levels of cache. The fastest cache with the smallest capacity is Level 1 cache. The CPU will optimise its use of the fastest cache before using the next level, or using **Random Access Memory** (**RAM**), in order to improve performance speed.

EMBEDDED SYSTEMS

An **embedded system** is used to control the function of electronic devices such as those commonly found in the home. They often don't need a full operating system since they perform limited and very specific tasks with their input frequently controlled by a button press or switch.

Embedded systems must be reliable since they cannot be modified once manufactured. The program that controls them is held in **Read Only Memory** (**ROM**).

Examples include air conditioning or heating systems, radio alarm clocks, washing machines, fridges, microwave ovens and digital cameras.

Jonny says that his car's satnav is an embedded system. State whether he is correct and explain your answer. [3]

Yes, he is correct.[1] It has one dedicated function[1] with simple controls. The user cannot change the software held in ROM within the embedded system.[1] The user cannot run other general software on it.[1]

Number of cores

A processor may contain more than one **core**. Each core can process one operation per clock cycle. A dual- or quad-core processor will be able to perform 2 or 4 operations simultaneously (for example, run two programs simultaneously), but only if the software it is running is designed for multi-core processors.

Amy's computer has a 4.5 GHz, dual core processor.

(a) How many cycles is a 4.5 GHz, dual core processor theoretically able to perform each second? [1]

(b) Explain why a computer with a dual core processor may not be twice as fast as a single core processor with the same clock speed. [2]

(a) 9 billion.[1]

(b) The software running on the computer may not be written to make the most efficient use of multiple cores.[1] Additional cores may be redundant if the software is only written for a single core[1] or if the output of one operation is required to perform the second operation[1] so they cannot be processed simultaneously[1].

CPU

Dual Core

Quad Core

Octa Core

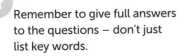

Remember to give full answers to the questions – don't just list key words.

PRIMARY STORAGE (MEMORY)

The need for primary storage

Main memory or **RAM** (**Random Access Memory**) is required to **temporarily store** the **programs**, **instructions** and **data** the computer needs whilst it is in operation. These are copied from the hard disk into main memory when they are required because it would be too slow to access everything directly from the hard disk. For even faster access, the most frequently used program instructions and data are held in **cache**.

RAM and ROM

RAM is the computer's temporary working memory. It is **volatile** which means it gets wiped as soon as the power is switched off. **ROM** (**Read Only Memory**) stores instructions and data that never need to be changed, such as the computer's start-up instructions so that it knows what to do when you push the 'on' button. ROM is **non-volatile**. As it is read-only, you cannot overwrite its contents once it has been set by the manufacturer.

RAM	ROM
Volatile – All data is lost when the power is turned off	Non-volatile – Data is permanently retained without power
Used for the computer's working memory for instructions, programs and data	Used for the computer's start-up instructions and in embedded systems
Can be written to, and read from	Read only, so cannot be written to

 Explain questions such as 'Explain why this is the most appropriate...' are not just a list of benefits. You should identify the benefits but then expand on each one, whilst also applying it to the scenario or context in the question.

1. Abeel had a power cut whilst working on a spreadsheet document. He said that he lost the entire document but could still open the spreadsheet program when the power came back on.

   Explain why this was the case for Abeel. [2]

   The spreadsheet program was stored on the hard drive and copied to RAM / main memory while the program was in use.[1] The document was created and stored in RAM[1], and disappeared because it was never saved[1]. If the document had been saved, it would have been copied to the hard disk[1].

2. An increase in RAM capacity can improve the speed of your computer.

   Explain why increased ROM size would not have the same effect. [2]

   ROM is only required to be as large as the start-up instructions inside it.[1] Any additional space will make no difference.[1] New files cannot be written into new space as it is read-only.[1]

1.2.1

VIRTUAL MEMORY

Virtual memory is used when there simply isn't enough space in RAM for all of the programs and data you are currently working on.

A small section of the hard disk is reserved to act like RAM. When the program in virtual memory is needed, it is swapped with something else in RAM. This swapping may cause your computer to noticeably slow down since access to the hard disk isn't nearly as fast as RAM.

Here, Windows, Word and a Word document are opened and loaded into RAM from the hard disk. This fills up the available RAM completely. If Excel is then required, the CPU must first move Word out of RAM into virtual memory to free up enough space for Excel.

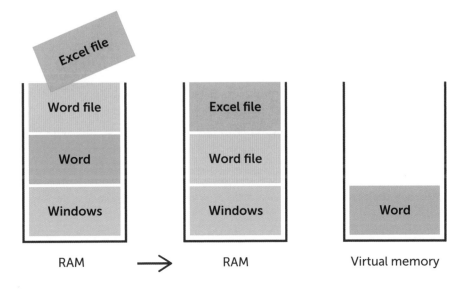

Imagine what happens when you put some revision material on your floor when you run out of desk space. Access to it gets slower.

Explain why getting more RAM would be preferable to using virtual memory. [2]

Access to data already in RAM is much faster than having to swap other programs in and out of RAM before accessing them.[1] Constantly swapping programs and data between RAM and the hard disk (virtual memory) can cause disk thrashing[1] which takes time and decreases performance[1]. Reading data from a hard disk is much slower than from RAM.[1]

SECONDARY STORAGE

The need for secondary storage

Secondary storage includes **hard disks** (internal and external), **USB flash drives**, **CDs** and other portable storage devices. We need secondary storage for longer term storage of files and data because it is non-volatile, which means your data will not disappear when the power is turned off. External devices are portable and may have very large capacities.

Applications of storage media

Solid state drives (**SSDs**) require very little power and create little heat owing to the lack of moving parts. This makes them suitable for laptop and tablet devices commonly used on the go. The lack of moving parts also means they are very thin and reliable – perfect for small portable devices with built-in storage such as cameras and smartphones. SSDs are also used in desktop and larger computers and are replacing hard disks in mass storage facilities as they can be 100 times faster than hard disks and do not require expensive cooling equipment.

Hard disk drives (**HDDs**) are commonly found in desktop computers, but SSDs are frequently used for some applications such as the operating system and other software that needs to execute as fast as possible. **CDs** and **DVDs** are useful for archiving data in the short to medium term with a life expectancy of 10–25 years. **Memory sticks** may be more effective for more regular backup of small files as they are more durable.

1. Explain why secondary storage is necessary in most
   smartphones.   [2]
2. Explain why a solid state drive is commonly chosen for
   smartphone storage.   [4]

   1. Secondary storage is non-volatile.[1] Without secondary storage, you are not able to store photos, video and files for another session once the power has been switched off[1].

   2. Solid state storage is durable with no moving parts[1], so it will be more robust if dropped[1]. It is reliable which will mean few repairs or inconvenient faults.[1] It is portable and lightweight and takes up little physical space[1], reducing the physical device size[1], ease of use[1] and weight[1] of the phone for the user. Solid state storage has very efficient power consumption[1] providing longer battery life for mobile devices[1].

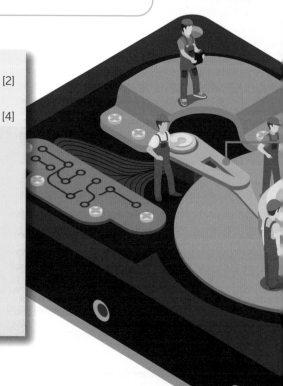

The advantages and disadvantages of different storage devices

	Optical	Magnetic (HDD)	Solid state (SSD)
Capacity	From 650 MB (CD) to 50 GB (Blu-Ray Dual layer)	Up to 16 TB	Up to 4 TB for an SSD, or 256 GB for a Flash USB Memory stick
Speed	Up to 50 MB/s. Limited as there are moving parts	Up to 200 MB/s. Moving parts means relatively slow speed compared to SSD	Up to 3.5 GB/s for an SSD as there are no moving parts
Portability	Highly portable and lightweight	Internal drives are not portable. External drives are similar in size to a large smartphone	Flash drives and memory cards are highly portable. Internal SSDs are not intended to be portable but are very lightweight for use in laptops and tablet computers
Durability	Susceptible to scratches and will degrade over time and with exposure to sunlight	Good when not in use. Can be affected by magnetic fields and heat	Extremely durable
Reliability	Good in the medium term	Very reliable	Extremely reliable
Cost	50 GB for 45p	8 TB for £120	4 TB for £400

Justify each choice on grounds of two or three of the characteristics: capacity, speed, portability, durability, reliability and cost.

3. Justify a different storage device for each of the following applications.
   (a) A database server in a busy office. [3]
   (b) Event photographs sent by post to a company from a photographer. [3]
   (c) Regular transfer of files between home and a place of work. [3]

(a) Hard disk drives (HDD)[1] have very high capacity[1] and are relatively inexpensive compared to SSDs[1]. Fast, durable and reliable.[1] (Or, could justify SSD on grounds of speed, capacity, reliability.)

(b) CD or DVD.[1] Very inexpensive, costing only a few pence[1], easy to post[1], and will only be used once[1].

(c) USB flash drive.[1] Has sufficient capacity and speed for this purpose[1], very portable[1], durable[1], reliable[1] and inexpensive[1]. (Accept valid alternatives.)

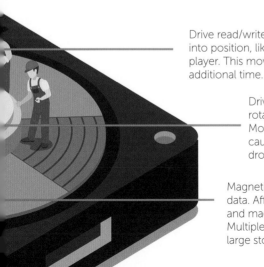

Drive read/write head moves into position, like a record player. This movement takes additional time.

Drive spindle rotates disk. Moving parts cause issues if dropped.

Magnetic platter stores data. Affected by heat and magnetic fields. Multiple platters provide large storage volume.

EXAMINATION PRACTICE

1   Which **one** of the following devices is both an input and an output device?   [1]
    A   Scanner
    B   Web cam
    C   Mouse
    D   Touch screen

2. Which **one** of the following defines the role of the accumulator in a CPU?   [1]
    A   It acts as a large cache memory
    B   It is a register in which the results of calculations are temporarily stored
    C   It regulates the clock speed
    D   It holds the address of the next instruction to be performed

3. Which of the following best describes the use of virtual memory?   [1]
    A   An area of internal HDD or SSD storage used when RAM is full
    B   Used as offsite storage using a Cloud provider
    C   A writeable CD
    D   A solid state USB drive frequently removed from the computer

4. Lindy has a new computer with 6 MB cache and 8 GB of RAM.
    (a) Explain how the use of cache can increase a computer's processing speed.   [3]
    (b) Give **one** reason why computers have less cache memory than random access memory.   [1]

5. State **one** use of a ROM memory chip.   [1]

6. Two components within a modern CPU are the Control Unit (CU) and the Arithmetic Logic Unit (ALU).
    Describe the function of each.
    (a) Control Unit: [2]
    (b) Arithmetic Logic Unit: [2]

7. Two CPUs run at the same clock speed but one appears to be faster than the other.
    Explain **two** reasons why this might be possible.   [4]

8. A tablet computer is being designed with 256 GB storage.
    Suggest **one** suitable storage device. Justify your answer.   [3]

UNITS OF DATA STORAGE

Bit	Nibble	Byte	Kilobyte	Megabyte	Gigabyte	Terabyte	Petabyte
0 or 1	4 Bits	8 Bits	1000 Bytes	1000 kB	1000 MB	1000 GB	1000 TB

Switches

A computer is made up of billions of **switches**, each with two states - an off position (represented by a 0) and an on position (represented by a 1). This is known as **binary**. All data therefore needs to be converted into binary before it can be processed by a computer.

By placing two or more switches in a row, you double the number of combinations of 1s and 0s with each additional switch.

Work out the following:

(a) Calculate the number of 650 MB CDs required to store 2 GB of images. Show your working. [1]

(b) Calculate the total capacity of a server with 4 x 2.5 TB hard disk drives. [1]

(c) Calculate the total storage requirement for a database of 5,000 customer records each of 1.5 kB each. Give your answer in MB. Show your working. [2]

(a) 2 GB = 2000 MB. 2000/650 = 3.08 (>3). Therefore 4 CDs will be required. [1]

(b) 10 TB [1]

(c) 5000 × 1.5 kB = 7500 kB [1] = 7.5 MB. [1]

Look at a variety of on / off (1 or 0) switches on electrical items.

What do you think this symbol represents?

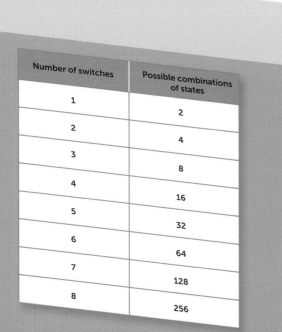

Number of switches	Possible combinations of states
1	2
2	4
3	8
4	16
5	32
6	64
7	128
8	256

BINARY ⇄ DENARY CONVERSION

Converting binary numbers into positive denary whole numbers

Our denary or decimal system has a base of 10 digits 0–9. Binary has a base of just 2 digits, 0 and 1. Instead of a representing three-digit numbers with a ones, tens and hundreds column for example, binary represents them with a ones column, a twos column and a fours column.

To make a conversion from binary to denary, add the place value headers where there is a 1.

128	64	32	16	8	4	2	1
0	1	1	0	1	0	0	1
	1×64 +	1×32 +		1×8 +			1×1 = 105

Converting positive denary whole numbers to binary

To convert the denary number 87 into binary, start with the **most significant bit** (left-hand end of the table below). Does 128 go into 87? If not, add a 0 in that column. Does 64 go into 87? Yes, it does, so add a 1 to the column and calculate the remainder, 23. 32 does not go into 23 so add a 0 to the next column. 16 goes into 23 with a remainder of 7. 8 won't go into 7 so add a 0 next. 4 will go with a remainder of 3. 2 will go into 3 with a remainder of 1 and 1 goes into 1 so add a 1 to each of the last three columns.

Note that the maximum value that can be held with eight bits where all bits = 1, is 255.

A binary number with a 1 in the least significant bit (far right-hand position) will always be odd.

128	64	32	16	8	4	2	1
0	1	0	1	0	1	1	1
	r23		r7		r3	r1	

1. Convert the following denary numbers to binary:
   (a) 138 [1]
   (b) 57 [1]
2. Convert the following binary numbers to denary:
   (a) 0110 1101 [1]
   (b) 1110 0110 [1]

   1. (a) 1000 1010[1], (b) 0011 1001[1]
   2. (a) 109[1], (b) 230[1]

Counting in binary

0	0000		8	1000
1	0001		9	1001
2	0010		10	1010
3	0011		11	1011
4	0100		12	1100
5	0101		13	1101
6	0110		14	1110
7	0111		15	1111

ADDING BINARY INTEGERS

Binary addition is done in the same way that denary numbers might be added together.

The rules are as follows:

0 + 0 = 0
0 + 1 or 1 + 0 = 1
1 + 1 = 0 carry a 1
1 + 1 + 1 = 1 carry a 1

> Note that in the same way as the denary values 00028 and 28 represent the same value, the binary value 00011100 is the same as 11100. Any leading zeros (left-hand side) are ignored.

Carry	1	1	1	1		1			Check
	0	1	0	1	1	0	1	1	91
+	0	0	1	1	1	0	1	0	58
	1	0	0	1	0	1	0	1	149

Overflow

Overflow occurs when the result of adding two binary numbers is greater than the number of bits allowed, (eight in this example). The maximum value that can be held with 8 bits is 255. (In practice, integers would be held typically in 32 bits.)

Consider the following example to illustrate this:

1						1	1		Check
	1	1	0	0	0	0	0	1	193
+	1	0	0	0	1	0	1	1	139
1	0	1	0	0	1	1	0	0	332

> 1. Add the following binary numbers, leaving the answer as binary numbers.
>   (a) 0011 1011 + 1000 0110   [1]
>   (b) 1001 1100 + 0111 1110   [1]
> 2. Explain the problem that would occur in part 1(b) if the result was to be stored as an 8-bit number.   [2]
>
> *1. (a) 1100 0001[1], (b) 1 0001 1010[1]*
>
> *2. Overflow error[1] since the total was more than 11111111[1] (255 in denary.)*

HEXADECIMAL ⇄ BINARY CONVERSION

The **hexadecimal** number system uses a base of 16 instead of 2 or 10. Given that we only have ten digits 0–9 in our system, the additional six number 10–15 in the hexadecimal system are represented by the letters A–F.

Denary	Binary	Hex
0	0000	0
1	0001	1
2	0010	2
3	0011	3
4	0100	4
5	0101	5
6	0110	6
7	0111	7

Denary	Binary	Hex
8	1000	8
9	1001	9
10	1010	A
11	1011	B
12	1100	C
13	1101	D
14	1110	E
15	1111	F

One hexadecimal (or hex) number can represent one nibble of 4 bits. This is easier to remember than the binary representation.

Converting a binary number into hexadecimal

To convert the number 0100 1111 to hexadecimal, first split the eight-bit binary number into two nibbles of four bits each. Convert each nibble separately and join the results.

0100	1111		01001111
4	15 (F)	=	4F

Some further examples are:
1011 0101 = **B5** and 1100 1101 = **CD**

1. Convert the following binary values into hexadecimal: [3]
   (a) 0110 1011
   (b) 0000 1001
   (c) 1111 1111
2. Convert the following hexadecimal values into binary: [3]
   (a) 48
   (b) 6A
   (c) F9

1. (a) 6B[1], (b) 09[1], (c) FF[1]
2. (a) 0100 1000[1],
   (b) 0110 1010[1],
   (c) 1111 1001[1]

Converting a hexadecimal number into binary

Convert each hex character into a four-bit binary value and join them to make a byte.

7	E (14)		7E
0111	1110	=	01111110

Further examples are: B9 = 1011 1001 and DA = 1101 1010.

HEXADECIMAL ⇄ DENARY CONVERSION

To convert between **hexadecimal** and **denary**, you need to remember that hex has a base of 16, as opposed to our denary number system that has a base of 10. This means that instead of 1s and 10s, you have 1s and 16s.

Converting a hexadecimal number into denary

Multiply the hexadecimal digits by their column place values 16 and 1, then add the results.

To convert the hex number 5B to decimal:

16	1		
5	B	(B = 11)	
(5 × 16)	(11 × 1)		
80	11	80 + 11 =	91

Here are some further examples:
Hexadecimal 88 = denary **136** and hexadecimal FA = denary **250**

Converting a denary number into hexadecimal

First work out how many 16s go into the number. This is the first hex digit. Then take the remainder and use this as the second hex digit. To convert 195 to hex:

195 / 16 = 12 remainder 3
12 = **C**
3 = **3**   so 195 in denary is **C3** in
            hexadecimal

Here are some further examples:
Denary 67 = hexadecimal **43**
Denary 219 = hexadecimal **DB**

---

1. Convert the following hexadecimal values
   into denary: [3]
   (a) 9F   (b) C2   (c) 63
2. Convert the following denary values
   into hexadecimal: [3]
   (a) 63   (b) 160   (c) 15

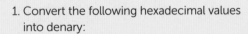

1. (a) 9F = 159[1], (b) C2 = 194[1], (c) 63 = 99[1]
2. (a) 3F[1], (b) A0[1] (c) F[1]

BINARY SHIFTS

A **binary shift** moves all of the bits in a given binary number either to the left or the right by a given number of places. All of the empty spaces are then filled with zeros.

A shift of one place to the left will have the following effect:

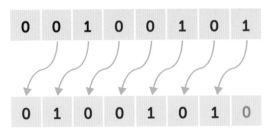

Effects of shifts

A shift to the left will multiply a binary number by 2. Two shifts left would therefore multiply a number by 4. Each shift right would divide a number by 2. Similarly, a shift left in denary of the number 17 becomes 170 and has therefore been multiplied by its base of 10.

An issue with precision occurs where odd numbers are divided since a standard byte cannot represent fractional numbers. Consider the following shift of three places to the right:

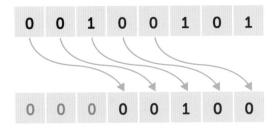

The original binary value was equal to denary 37. A right shift should divide this by 8 (or divide by 2, three times). 37 / 8 = 4.625. However, the resulting binary converted to denary is 4.

---

1. Complete a 2-place shift to the right on the binary number 11010110. [1]

2. Explain the effect of performing a right shift of two places on the binary number 11010110. [2]

3. Explain the effect of performing a left shift of 1 place on the binary number 11010110. [2]

   1. 0011 0101[1]

   2. Each shift right will divide the number by 2, so a two-place shift right will divide the number by 4[1]. However, if the shift results in a 1 being lost at the right hand end, the results will lose precision[1]. This is demonstrated in this question. 1101 0110 is 214 in denary. Dividing that by 4 = 53.5. The shifted result 0011 0101 however is only 53 in denary.

   3. Shifting one place left multiplies the number by 2.[1] However this will cause an overflow error[1] for the given number, as 9 bits would be needed for the result, which is greater than 255 (1 byte).[1]

CHARACTERS

Each **character** on the keyboard has a binary code which is transmitted to the computer each time a key is pressed. Some of the characters and their codes, known as the **character set**, for the standard keyboard are given below. The **ASCII** character set consists of 128 characters, each using 7 bits to uniquely represent them. ASCII stands for American Standard Code for Information Interchange.

ASCII	DEC	Binary	ASCII	DEC	Binary	ASCII	DEC	Binary	ASCII	DEC	Binary
NULL	000	000 0000	space	032	010 0000	@	064	100 0000	`	096	110 0000
SOH	001	000 0001	!	033	010 0001	A	065	100 0001	a	097	110 0001
STX	002	000 0010	"	034	010 0010	B	066	100 0010	b	098	110 0010
ETX	003	000 0011	#	035	010 0011	C	067	100 0011	c	099	110 0011
EOT	004	000 0100	$	036	010 0100	D	068	100 0100	d	100	110 0100
ENQ	005	000 0101	%	037	010 0101	E	069	100 0101	e	101	110 0101
ACK	006	000 0110	&	038	010 0110	F	070	100 0110	f	102	110 0110
BEL	007	000 0111	'	039	010 0111	G	071	100 0111	g	103	110 0111
BS	008	000 1000	(	040	010 10..	H	072	100 1000	h		110 1000

Using the ASCII table in programming

The character codes are grouped and run in sequence; i.e. if a capital 'A' is 65 then 'B' must be 66 and so on. The pattern applies to other groupings such as lowercase characters and digits. For example, '1' is 49, so '5' must be 53. Also, '3' < '4' and 'a' < 'b'.

Notice that the ASCII code value for '7' (011 0111) is different from the pure binary value for 7 (000 0111). This is why you can't calculate with numbers that have been input as strings.

Character sets

A character set consists of all the letters, numbers and special characters that can be recognised by a computer system. The ASCII character set uses 7 bits and consists of 128 characters as shown in the table above.

Extended ASCII uses 8 bits rather than 7. This allows up to 256 characters to be represented. Additional characters in the set include symbols, common foreign language characters and mathematical characters for example, ©, €, é and ¼. 7-bit codes translate into 8-bit codes directly using an additional 0 as the most significant (leftmost) bit. For example, 'a' translates from 110 0001 to 0110 0001.

Unicode uses 16 bits per character, and can represent 65,536 different characters. This is enough to represent all of the characters in most international languages including those in Russian, Chinese, Arabic and emojis ☺.

Use the ASCII table for this question.
1. Show how the word CAGE is represented in ASCII. Give your answer in binary. [1]
2. State how many bytes would be used to store the phrase "BIRD CAGE" using extended 8-bit ASCII. [1]

1. Each letter would be represented in one byte by its binary ASCII value written in the same order that the characters are entered, e.g.

1000011 1000001 1000111 1000101[1]

2. 9 bytes.[1] (The Space character has the code 32 and occupies one byte.)

IMAGES

Similar to a mosaic, a **bitmap** image is made up of picture elements or **pixels**. A pixel represents the smallest identifiable area of an image, each appearing as a square with a single colour.

Colour depth

The first symbol below is represented in black and white using a series of binary codes. 0 = black and 1 = white.

0	1	1	1
1	0	1	0
1	1	0	0
1	0	0	0

11	11	11	00
10	10	10	10
10	10	01	10
10	10	01	10

Given that only 1 bit per pixel is available, only two colours, black and white, can be represented. The full image would have a size of 16 bits or 2 bytes. If the number of bits per pixel is increased, more colours can be represented. In the second example, four colours can be represented as the **colour depth** (also known as **bit depth**), or bits per pixel has been doubled to two. This will also double the file size.

Number of colours		Colour depth
2 colours	2^1 colours	1 bit per pixel required
4 colours	2^2 colours	2 bit per pixel required
8 colours	2^3 colours	3 bit per pixel required
16 colours	2^4 colours	4 bit per pixel required

1. Study the bitmap images above.

(a) Give the binary representation for the top row of the second, four-colour example. [2]

(b) State the colour depth of an image if a palette of 256 colours per pixel is required. [1]

(c) State the effect on file size on the first 4x4 pixel symbol above of increasing the numbers of available colours to 256. [1]

(a) 11 11[1] 11 00[1]. One mark per correct pair.

(b) 8 bits per pixel.[1] (2^8 = 256)

(c) The file size would increase[1] to 1 byte per pixel, or 16 bytes for the whole icon, from 16 bits or 2 bytes[1].

Effect of colour depth and resolution

As the number of bits per pixel increases (the **colour depth** or **bit depth**), so does the quality of the image as you are able to more accurately represent the full range of colours visible to the naked eye. However, this significantly increases the **file size**.

| 2 colours | 4 colours | 8 colours | 16 colours | 256 colours | 65.536 colours | 16.7m colours |

Simply increasing the number of pixels in an image will also increase its size. An 8 x 8 pixel icon will be four times larger than a 4 x 4 pixel icon with the same colour depth.

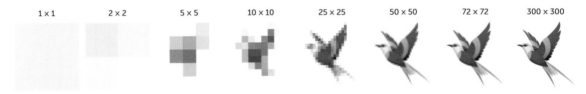

| 1 × 1 | 2 × 2 | 5 × 5 | 10 × 10 | 25 × 25 | 50 × 50 | 72 × 72 | 300 × 300 |

The density of pixels in the same sized area defines the **resolution**. More pixels per inch (**PPI**) will smooth the edges and improve the overall quality. This will increase the size of the image file, making it possible to enlarge the image without a visible loss of quality.

Metadata

Metadata is data about data. The data stored in a file alongside the actual file data identifies, for example, the type of image, when it was created and who it was created by, the image dimensions and the colour depth.

2. An image has 1000 x 1000 pixels and a colour depth of 24 bits.

(a) State the file size of the image in MB. [2]

(b) Calculate how many colours are available for each pixel if an image has a colour depth of 8 bits. [1]

(c) Metadata often accompanies image data.
   Give **two** examples of metadata. [2]

*(a) 3 MB.[1] 1000 x 1000 * 24 / 8 = 3,000 kB[1] or 3 MB.*

(b) 2^8 = 256 colours.[1]

(c) Examples include height[1], width[1], geolocation[1], file type[1], date created[1]. Cannot accept file size or file name.

SOUND

Analogue sounds must be digitally recorded in binary. In order to record sound, the **amplitude** or height of the soundwave emitted must be measured and recorded at regular intervals. How often the height is recorded (the **frequency** or **sample rate**), and the accuracy to which the height is recorded (the **bit depth** or **sample resolution**) affect the quality of the recorded sound when played back and the file size of the recording. The **duration** of the recording will also affect the file size.

The **sample rate** is measured in **hertz**. CD quality playback is recorded at 44.1 KHz.

Examples A and B show how the digitally represented wave more accurately follows the analogue sound wave form with a greater **bit depth**.

Examples B and C show how waves recorded at identical resolutions are much more accurately represented with a greater number of **samples per second**.

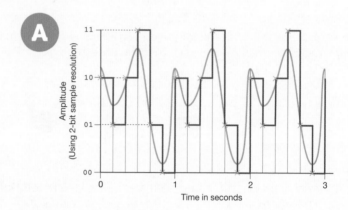

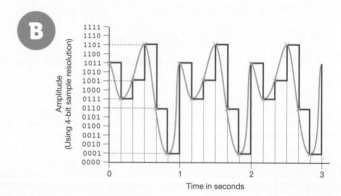

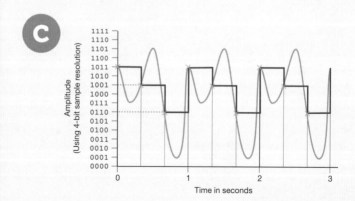

Look at Examples A, B and C.

(a) Give the binary representation for the first six samples taken in the first second of recording in Example A. [2]

(b) State how many different amplitudes or wave heights could be recorded if the bit depth was 8. [1]

(c) State the sample frequency in hertz of Example C. [1]

(d) Calculate the file size in bytes of a message alert tone lasting 3 seconds, using a sample rate of 8 kHz and an 8-bit sample resolution. [1]

(a) 10, 01, 10[1], 11, 01, 00[1]

(b) 2^8 = 256[1]

(c) 3 Hz[1] (3 samples per second.)

(d) 8,000 samples per second, taken at 8 bits each = 64 kilobits / 8 = 8 kB x 3 seconds duration = 24 kB.[1]

COMPRESSION

Compression software uses **algorithms** to remove repeated or unnecessary data. This reduces the size of a file on disk, and of large files sent by email where there are maximum attachment limits. It is also useful for streaming data over the Internet and for images and video embedded within websites as smaller files will be transmitted in less time, meaning the streamed video content or website takes less time to download. A **bitmap** (**.bmp**) image is uncompressed.

Type	Lossy compression	Lossless compression
Formats	JPG, MP3, WMV, MPG	TIF, PDF, GIF, PNG, MOV, ZIP
Examples	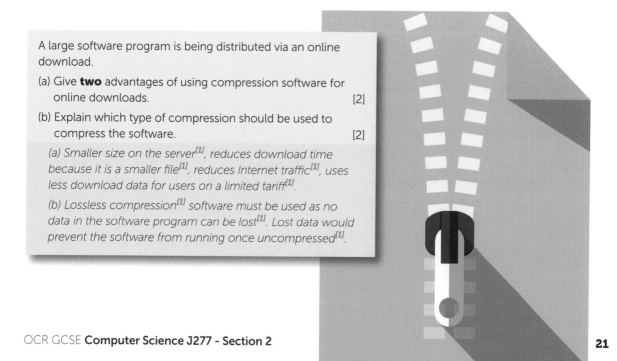	
Advantages	Smallest file sizes, least transmission time, reduces Internet traffic and collisions	Original quality is preserved / no information or data is lost
Disadvantages	Detail is permanently lost	Less significant reduction in file size
Example uses	Music streaming, online images and video, image libraries on devices or in the cloud	Text documents, electronic books, high resolution print documents

A large software program is being distributed via an online download.

(a) Give **two** advantages of using compression software for online downloads. [2]

(b) Explain which type of compression should be used to compress the software. [2]

(a) Smaller size on the server[1], reduces download time because it is a smaller file[1], reduces Internet traffic[1], uses less download data for users on a limited tariff[1].

(b) Lossless compression[1] software must be used as no data in the software program can be lost[1]. Lost data would prevent the software from running once uncompressed[1].

EXAMINATION PRACTICE

1. Calculate the following:
   (a) The number of bytes in a 4.5 kB text document. [1]
   (b) The number of megabytes in a 2 GB sound recording. [1]
   (c) The denary number 28 can be represented in binary using 8 bits.
      (i) Convert denary 28 to binary. [1]
      (ii) Explain how a binary shift could be used to divide the number by 2. [1]

2. Standard SMS text message technology permits 160 characters per message using the 8-bit ASCII character set.
   (a) Explain what is meant by a character set. [1]
   (b) Using this technology, state how many bytes are used to send a message of 160 characters. [1]
   (c) The Unicode character for the Chinese, Japanese, Korean (CJK) symbol for 'Hi' is 嗨.
      The hexadecimal character code for 嗨 is 55E8.
      (i) Complete the conversion of 55E8 into binary below. [2]

Hex:	5	5	E	8
Binary:	0101	0101		

   (ii) Explain why smartphones that can send text messages in multiple languages would use Unicode instead of ASCII as their character set. [2]

3. A bitmap image with a colour depth of 1 bit has been created.
   (a) Convert the following binary data into an image with a resolution of 5 x 5 pixels, where 0 represents black and 1 represents white:
   00100 10101 10001 00000 10101

   (b) Justify an appropriate compression method for an image designed for use on a website. [4]
   The file size of the image as stored on a computer shows as 17 bytes.
   (c) Explain what additional data may be included with this file to increase the file size beyond the 25 bits required to display the raw image. [2]

4. Anil has made a sound recording of a short piece of music. The quality of the playback is poor. Anil believes this is to do with the bit depth.
   (a) State what is meant by bit depth. [1]
   (b) Explain how the bit depth could affect the quality of a sound recording. [2]
   Anil says that the file size of the recording needs to be below his email attachment limit.
   (c) Describe **one** factor besides sample resolution which will affect the file size of Anil's recording. [2]

NETWORKS

There are two main types of network. A **LAN (Local Area Network)** and a **WAN (Wide Area Network)**. A WAN connects LANs together to form larger networks.

LAN	WAN
Operates on a single site or within a single organisation across buildings close to each other	Used to connect computers together over large distances, often nationally or internationally
Uses its own Ethernet hardware and cabling to transmit data	Uses third party or external hardware and cabling, including satellites, phone lines and the Internet
Examples include small company networks and home networks	Examples include the multi-national banking network and the Internet

Greater bandwidth allows more data to travel along a cable simultaneously. Imagine a motorway with either 4 or 8 lanes – cars (data packets) go no faster with more lanes, there are just more of them reaching their destination within the same time period.

Network performance

Network performance is affected by the amount of data being transmitted across the network. In a LAN, if two or more devices are attempting to transmit at the same time along the same channel, **data collisions** occur, and the data has to be retransmitted. (This is like two people talking on the telephone at the same time.)

The **bandwidth** of the transmission medium affects how much data can travel at once. Fibre optic cable has a much higher bandwidth than copper cabling and can transmit much more data simultaneously. Data is transmitted using light signals in fibre optic cables and electrical signals in copper cables. **Signal strength** deteriorates with greater **distance**.

1. Describe **two** factors which affect the performance of a network. [6]

   The number of active devices[1] will increase the number of data collisions[1]. Two data packets sent simultaneously may collide[1], causing an error and retransmission[1].

   In a wireless network, interference from other devices nearby[1] such as Bluetooth devices or microwave ovens[1] disrupts the signal and the connection becomes unreliable[1], causing delays and unexpected disconnections[1].

   Alternative answers include bandwidth / type of cabling / performance of the server / signal strength / distance from Wi-Fi access point.

2. An office has a network router and Ethernet points throughout. Each computer is connected to a switch with a wired Ethernet connection. Mobile devices are connected to a wireless access point using Wi-Fi. State whether the network is a LAN or WAN based on this information.

   Justify your answer. [3]

   This is a LAN network[1] because it is situated across a small area within the same building[1]. It also uses its own hardware and cabling[1] to connect each computer without the use of any third-party infrastructure[1].

NETWORK HARDWARE

A LAN requires different **hardware** components to connect **stand-alone** computers together.

Wireless access point – also referred to as a wireless AP. Creates a wireless network using radio waves through which a Wi-Fi enabled device can connect to communicate with the network or the Internet.

Switch – is used to connect devices on a LAN. It receives data packets and forwards them to the correct device using their unique individual **Media Access Control** (**MAC**) address.

Router – directs data packets from one router to another between start and end points on a network. They sit between LANs and WANs to join them together with a public IP address for the WAN and a private IP address for the LAN. Any local data is passed on to the Internet by the router. Any inbound data from the Internet is received and directed internally.

NIC (**Network Interface Controller/Card**) – a hardware component required to connect any device to a network. Wired and wireless versions are available. Nearly all new computers have a NIC built directly into the motherboard.

Describe **two** advantages and **two** disadvantages of the star topology. [8]

Advantages: Very reliable[1] as if one cable fails, the other nodes will be unaffected.[1] Data collisions can be avoided[1] by using this topology with a switch. This improves network performance.[1]

Disadvantages: A cable is required to connect every computer[1] which can be expensive[1] and requires a switch to direct transmission to the correct networked device[1]. If the switch fails[1], all devices on the network will lose their network connection[1].

Exam tip: This question requires 4 points for 8 marks. Give two advantages and disadvantages and then give a reason why each point is valid. Using words such as 'because', 'so' and 'as' will help you justify each response.

TOPOLOGIES

There are two main networking structures or topologies in use today. These are **star** and **mesh** topologies.

Star networks

Star networks are most commonly used in businesses and organisations where performance and security is essential. They are also found in smaller offices and home networks owing to their simplicity. Each device on the network is connected to a central **switch** which directs transmissions to the correct device using its unique **MAC address**. Some home routers will also have switch and wireless access point capabilities.

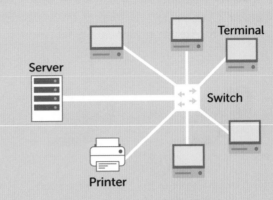

Mesh networks

Mesh networks can be used to connect small offices or entire cities. Wireless examples are most common, providing very large networks supporting traffic management and home automation systems. In a full mesh topology, every node is connected to every other node. Each node sends its own signals and in addition, relays data from other nodes.

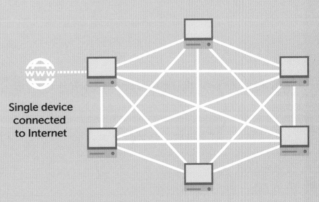

More common is the partial mesh topology, where some of the devices may be connected to only one or two others. This is less costly and reduces redundancy.

Advantages of mesh networks	Disadvantages of mesh networks
• Highly robust as the network will automatically find a different route if there is a fault with one connection or node.	• The network is very expensive to set up as it is difficult to establish the connections.
• Data can be transmitted from several devices simultaneously. The network can cope with high traffic.	• Self-maintenance and network administration is complex; it may be difficult to expand the network.
• Local networks run faster than in a star network because data does not have to travel via a central switch.	

CLIENT-SERVER NETWORKS

In a **client-server** network:

- The **server** is a powerful computer which provides services or resources required by its clients.
- A **client** is a computer which requests the services or resources provided by the server – you, as a user are most likely using a client computer on a school network that has many servers.

Depending on the purpose of the network, the server may provide different services:

| A file server will store or provide files upon client requests. | A mail server, for example, will filter spam, send or provide email when you want to read it via a client machine. | A web server will provide web pages at the request of the user's browser on the client computer. | A print server will queue print jobs requested by client computers and ensure that each job is sent to the correct printer. |

Advantages of a client server network	Disadvantages
<ul><li>Central storage of files so users can access them from any computer.</li><li>All client computers can search and update a central database to avoid multiple copies becoming out of sync.</li><li>Backups can be made centrally so that individuals do not need to back up their own client machines.</li><li>Security can be managed centrally using antivirus software on the server.</li><li>Software can be upgraded and installed centrally without having to visit each client machine.</li><li>Client machine usage and behaviour can be monitored to provide a history of use and to ensure correct procedures are followed.</li></ul>	<ul><li>Requires a costly maintenance team to manage the network and the server.</li><li>Too many client requests will degrade server performance.</li><li>If the server or its network connection go down then the service is lost for the whole network.</li></ul>

PEER-TO-PEER (P2P) NETWORKS

A **P2P network** has no central server. All nodes are equal and share resources such as files. P2P networks are commonly used in small offices or homes where it is not cost effective to have specialist network support and a server. Wired or wireless configurations may be used.

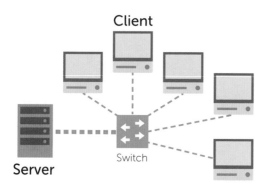

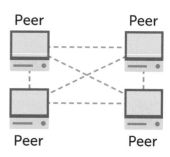

SprintCare is a small charity that uses several computers in a small office. The charity serves hundreds of local individuals using a database to store their details.

Discuss whether a client-server or a peer-to-peer network would be most appropriate for the charity. [8]

Storage and backup

A central backing store is available to all computers with a client-server network[v], whereas a peer-to-peer network distributes files across all computers[v]. Since the charity uses a database holding personal details of individuals, it would be better to keep this on a central server so that a single version remains up-to-date.[v] Central file storage also allows for central backup of all data.[v] A P2P network would require separate backups of each machine.[v]

Security

Security is easier to maintain with one central server responsible for everything.[v] A peer-to-peer network relies on each computer to monitor its own security.[v] The charity does not have many computers so it may be practical to maintain high levels of security with either choice of network.[v]

Reliability

A client-server network relies on the server to be switched on and connected.[v] If there are any faults or power failures with the server, the whole network would suffer.[v] In a P2P network, each individual device can transmit data across the network so a single cable or device failure will not affect the entire network.[v]

Suitability / complexity / maintenance

Installation and maintenance costs are greater for a client-server system[v], but overall it would be more secure and therefore appropriate for the charity[v]. Keeping the personal details of individuals secure is a legal requirement and of crucial importance.[v]

Marks are indicative only. Refer to the band descriptions and levels of response guidance for extended response questions on page 94.

THE INTERNET

The **Internet** is a global network of interconnected networks. The **World Wide Web** is all the web pages that are accessible via the Internet.

The role of a **Domain Name Server** is to convert a website address (**URL** e.g. www.google.co.uk) into an **IP address** (e.g. 172.217.14.195) so that a browser on a client machine can make a request to the correct server hosting that web page. If the DNS server does not have an entry for the domain name, it passes the request to another more authoritative DNS server. An error is sent back if no match is found.

> Be your own DNS! Try typing in 172.217.14.195 into a browser instead of a www.google.co.uk.

A web **hosting** company will host websites, files and databases. They will maintain high bandwidth connections, perform backups and keep the servers online 24 hours a day.

The **Cloud** is a term used for a file server accessible via the Internet. It is a remote server often owned by a third-party company which offers storage space for your files as well as backup and security services. Examples include Google Drive, OneDrive and DropBox.

Cloud advantages	Cloud disadvantages
• Flexible storage is offered so you can scale your requirements up or down overnight. • You do not need to purchase and maintain expensive hardware. • The Cloud storage provider is responsible for the security of your data and regular backups. • One cloud storage centre is more environmentally friendly than millions of individual servers. • You do not need any networking skills or maintenance workers.	• You need a reliable Internet connection to access services. • You have no direct control over the security of your data. • Keeping your data on another company's server may cause issues of ownership and legal implications within the Data Protection Act 2018. • You may be responsible for any data security breaches, even though you had no direct control over the security of the data.

ArcAccounts is a small accountancy firm. They are considering whether to move all their data from their own server to a Cloud-based service provider.

Discuss the issues the company should consider before making a decision. [6]

Arc Accounts will save money on in-house server maintenance staff[✓] and hardware replacements since this will be taken care of by the Cloud storage provider[✓]. Service and security will also be taken care of[✓] but ArcAccounts will still be responsible for any breaches or loss of data[✓]. They will need to consider the legal position in those cases and whether they want to lose that level of control over their own data.[✓] The potential costs of Cloud storage will increase as the volume of data stored increases[✓], but this allows for the company to grow without upgrading their own infrastructure[✓]. Staff may be able to access data from any computer in the world with an Internet connection via the Cloud[✓] so they can expand their company internationally[✓]. ArcAccounts will need a very reliable and fast Internet connection[✓] to ensure that their data is always available[✓]. This may need to be upgraded if they do not currently have good bandwidth.[✓]

Marks are indicative only. Refer to the band descriptions and levels of response guidance for extended response questions on page 94.

CONNECTING WIRED AND WIRELESS NETWORKS

Data may be transmitted across a network using a **wired** or **wireless** connection.

Wired transmission media

Network cabling includes **coaxial cable**, **twisted pair Ethernet cable** or **fibre optic cable**. Coaxial and Ethernet cables use copper wire. This is lower cost but has some disadvantages which fibre overcomes. Fibre optic cable transmits data as pulses of light through a single strand of glass fibre which can transmit large amounts of data over long distances and without interference.

Ethernet refers to a set of rules commonly used across Local Area Networks to govern how data is sent and received.

Wireless transmission media

Wi-Fi uses radio waves to transmit data. As long as a device has a Wireless NIC, it can connect to a wireless network. Like Ethernet, Wi-Fi has its own set of rules to manage data transmission.

Bluetooth® is a radio-wave technology commonly used to connect devices within 10 metres of each other. Common uses include hands-free phone kits and smart speakers.

	Wired	Wireless
Transmission speed	Fast and consistent transmission speed	Typically slower than cabled connections
Expansion of network	Costly to add extra devices as additional cabling and switches may be required	Easy to connect additional devices, for example mobile and IoT devices, but additional devices will share the available bandwidth and increase the traffic
Interference	Copper cable can be susceptible to electrical or magnetic interference. Fibre optic cable avoids this	Wireless signals can be reduced by walls and interference from other wireless devices. This affects the connection speed
Signal strength	Ethernet cable maintains a good strength up to 100m, fibre optic cable can be much longer	Wireless hotspots are limited to a very small local area and require repeater devices to expand the range
Security	Data sent along cables cannot be easily intercepted	Wi-Fi signals may be easily intercepted without adequate encryption security

Tick **one** box in each row of the table below to identify the most appropriate connection type for the given scenarios. [3]

Scenario	Wi-Fi	Ethernet
A customer seating area in a fast food restaurant	✓[1] *(portable devices)*	
A server connected to a school network		✓[1] *(high bandwidth)*
An old brick office building with very thick walls		✓[1] *(interference)*

ENCRYPTION

Encryption is the process of encoding data so that it cannot be easily understood if it is discovered , stolen or intercepted.

An original message or data set is known as **plaintext**. This is converted into **ciphertext** by encoding it using a mathematical encryption algorithm and key. Both the key and the algorithm are required to encode or decode data.

Simple encryption with a pre-shared key works like this:

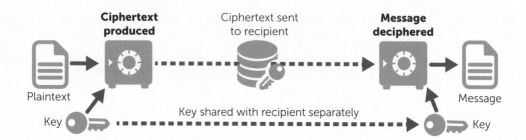

Caesar Cipher

A very primitive encryption algorithm was said to be invented by Julius Caesar. This is known as the Caesar cipher. This is a substitution cipher where each letter is replaced by another. The key in this instance would be 3 as A translates to D, three letters along the alphabet.

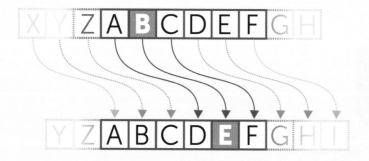

Jonny says that he has encrypted his work so that no one else can access it.

Explain why this isn't strictly true. [2]

Encryption encodes data making it unintelligible[1], but it could still be read, even if it would make no sense to anyone who did not have the decryption key[1].

Using the same principle, decode the message "LSPH JMVI" using a key of 4.

IP AND MAC ADDRESSING

An **IP address** is a unique **public address** for the **router** or gateway of a network. Data packets use this address to travel to the router, after which point they are directed using an internal (**private**) IP address within the network. Private addresses are not unique and the IP address of a portable device such as a laptop will change when it is moved, for example between towns.

An **IPv4** address is commonly four numbers (that can each be stored using 8 bits) each separated by a full stop. Your home router is likely to have the private IP address 192.168.0.1 for example. This system however is running out of possible addresses given the huge rise in networked devices. Owing to this, a new system called **IPv6** has been developed. This uses a 128-bit address which is usually represented in hexadecimal. This will provide enough address permutations to cater for all devices on the planet.

> IPv4 address: 212.58.244.66
> IPv6 address: 2001:0000:4136:e378:8000:63bf:3fff:fdd2
> MAC address: 30-A5-BD-6F-C4-63

A (Media Access Control) **MAC address** is a unique hexadecimal identification number assigned to every **Network Interface Card** used in networked devices. The IP address assigned to a computer or device may change, however, the MAC address will always be the same.

TCP/IP LAYERS

Transmission Control Protocol / Internet Protocol (TCP/IP) is a set of protocols operating on different layers.

Network **layers** provides a division of network functionality so that each layer can operate and be updated completely independently of any other layer.

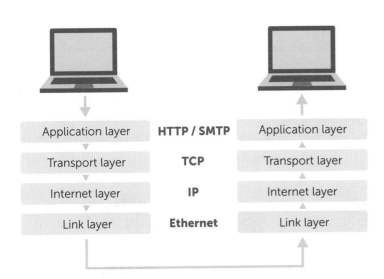

Describe **two** benefits of using protocol layers. [4]

Layers are self-contained with their own separate purposes[1] so manufacturers of hardware and software that operate on one layer need only be concerned with that layer's protocols[1]. This makes it possible for hardware from one manufacturer designed specifically to work on one particular layer to work with hardware produced for another layer by another manufacturer.[1] Software developers are also able to edit one layer without affecting others.[1] Layers provide more manageable divisions of work than one larger system.[1]

STANDARDS AND PROTOCOLS

Data transmission and communications **standards** have been developed to ensure that all connected devices can communicate seamlessly with each other using the same set of rules. A **protocol** is a set of **rules**. A network protocol defines the standards for data transmission.

The same principle applies to the use of standards in communications hardware manufacture and software development. A standard set of rules allows devices and programs produced by different companies to talk to each other. Examples include the speed of transmission, what to do in the case of collisions and how to check for errors.

The Highway Code establishes the rules for drivers in the UK. Without a standard, traffic would crash far more often. Likewise, English is a standard protocol for communication in the UK. Without a common language, communication would be very difficult. Imagine giving driving directions while blindfolded to someone using another language!

Different protocols are used for different purposes:

Protocol	Purpose	Key features
HTTP (Hypertext Transfer Protocol)	Used by a browser to access a webpage from a web server	Delivers web page data
HTTPS (Hypertext Transfer Protocol Secure)	As HTTP with encryption	Encrypts the data and uses a secure socket layer for greater protection
FTP (File Transfer Protocol)	Transmitting files between client and server computers	Used to upload and download files from a server
POP (Post Office Protocol)	Retrieving an email from an email server to your device	Deletes messages on the email server once they have been downloaded to a single device
IMAP (Internet Message Access Protocol)	Accessing email on a mail server via multiple devices	Maintains synchronisation of an email account across all devices
SMTP (Simple Mail Transfer Protocol)	Sending email messages between mail servers	Used for sending only

Bilal accesses his bank via an online banking website on his tablet computer.

Once logged in, Bilal can access his account data.

(a) Give a suitable protocol that could be used to transmit his account data. [1]

(b) Give **one** reason for your choice of protocol. [1]

(c) Bilal's bank sends him regular emails. Explain **two** protocols that are used in the sending and retrieval of email. [4]

(a) HTTPS[1], (b) HTTPS is a secure protocol that encrypts data in transmission.[1] (c) SMTP[1] is used to send the email to the bank's mail server.[1] This is passed to the client mail server.[1] POP or IMAP[1] is used to retrieve the email by Bilal's email client.[1]

 Hello Bonjour Hola Salve Olá

EXAMINATION PRACTICE

1. Tarun understands that protocols are used when he views a web page via the Internet.
   (a) State what is meant by a protocol in the context of data transmission. [1]
   (b) Explain why a standard protocol is necessary when transmitting data across a network. [2]
   (c) Explain how the Internet and the World Wide Web are used in the process of viewing
       a web page. [2]
   (d) State **one** protocol used when downloading a webpage from the Internet. [1]

2. David is exploring types of network with the idea of setting up a home network.
   (a) Explain the difference between a LAN and a WAN. [2]
   (b) David has discovered that he may require a router and a switch in a LAN.
       (i) State the role of a router. [1]
       (ii) State the role of a switch. [1]
   (c) In order to put his own website on the Internet, David understands he will need to find an
       Internet host.
       Explain what is meant by a host in this context. [2]

3. A travel speaker has been designed to use Bluetooth technology to connect to a nearby
   mobile phone.
   Explain why Bluetooth is a more appropriate connection for the speaker than a wired
   or Wi-Fi connection. [3]

4. Encryption is used by many organisations when communicating with their customers.
   (a) Explain what is meant by encryption. [2]
   (b) Explain why encryption is sometimes used when transmitting data over a network. [2]

5. Anderson Solutions is a rapidly growing software company with a head office in Newcastle.
   Several of their software engineers and programmers work from home. The company uses
   cloud storage for all their data.
   (a) Describe what is meant by cloud storage. [2]
   (b) Explain **three** advantages to the company of using cloud storage. [6]
   (c) Explain **one** disadvantage of using cloud storage. [2]

6. Su enters the URL www.bbc.co.uk into her browser. The website is hosted on a server with the
   IP address 199.232.56.81.
   (a) Explain how the website homepage is displayed on Su's browser. You should reference the
       website address, URL, IP address, DNS system and the website server in your answer. [5]
   (b) Give **two** advantages of dividing network functionality into layers. [2]

THREATS TO COMPUTER SYSTEMS AND NETWORKS

Forms of attack and defence

Malware:
Spyware and keyloggers

Software that hides on your computer recording your keystrokes to send back to a third party for analysis.

Anti-malware software

Data interception and theft

Data may be intercepted during transmission, but physical theft can occur where storage devices or data files are left insecurely.

Encryption / Physical locks / Biometrics

Shouldering

Looking over someone's shoulder when they enter a password or PIN.

Concealing your password or PIN entry / User access levels / User awareness

Malware:
Viruses

A virus is a program that is installed on your computer designed to replicate itself. Viruses cause harm to files and spread to other computers and devices.

Antivirus and anti-malware software / Don't click on links from unknown sources

Social engineering: Blagging

Dishonestly persuading someone to divulge personal or sensitive information by deception.

Security training

Social engineering: Phishing

Phishing emails redirect a user to a fake website where they trick the reader into divulging confidential information such as passwords that can be used fraudulently.

Network policy / Firewall / User awareness of phishing 'clues'

Hacking:
Denial of service attacks

Servers and devices are flooded with too many requests or packets, causing them to crash or become unusable.

Firewall

Hacking: Brute-force attacks

Automated or manual attempts to gain unauthorised access to secure areas by trying all possible password or key combinations.

Strong passwords with limited attempts / Penetration testing

SQL injection

Structured Query Language (**SQL**) is used to search databases. When data is entered into a web form, for example a username and a password, the web site will contact the database server to find the account details and display them. If, however, a hacker enters some malicious SQL into the password field of the web form instead of an actual password, it will modify the SQL that is executed. The example below would result in the unauthorised access of all of the records in the system since 1=1.

```
Select *
FROM usersList
WHERE (Username = $username)
AND (Password = $password) ;
```

→

```
Select *
FROM usersList
WHERE (Username = $username) OR (1=1)
AND (Password = $password) OR (1=1) ;
```

Give **two** methods of guarding against SQL injection attacks. [2]

You can guard against such well-known attacks by removing special characters (in SQL syntax) from data collection form fields[1], by using validation[1] and by limiting permissions to the database using different levels of access.[1] Penetration testing can help find remaining weaknesses.[1]

IDENTIFYING AND PREVENTING VULNERABILITIES

Penetration testing

Penetration testing, or **pen testing**, is used to find weaknesses in a system by employing someone to break in before a hacker has an opportunity to discover and exploit any vulnerabilities.

External pen testing aims to discover flaws and back doors into a system from outside the organisation – this might target servers and firewalls.

Internal pen testing puts the tester in the position of an employee who may already have a degree of access into the system. Just how much damage could a dishonest employee cause?

Anti-malware software protects a computer by preventing harmful programs from being installed on a computer.

If a virus is detected, the software will quarantine the file and remove it.

Anti-malware software should be kept constantly up-to-date to ensure the most recent threats are detected.

Firewalls are designed to prevent unauthorised access (hacking) to your computer. All data traffic is monitored as it passes through a hardware or software firewall which can block external attacks and access to banned websites from within the network.

Different **user access levels** can be granted to each employee of an organisation based on their needs. This limits the amount of data that a hacker is able to see depending on whose account may be compromised. Few employees will have access to everything.

Strong passwords should include numbers, upper- and lower-case letters and special characters, e.g. $, %, >. Passwords should never be written down and should be regularly changed.

Physical security includes locks on doors, server cabinets and security guards on the premises. Biometrics are commonly used as unique physical 'keys'.

Encryption is used to obscure data rendering it useless without the correct decryption algorithm and key.

Amber stores confidential information on the tablet computer that she uses for her job.

(a) Give **two** ways in which Amber could restrict unauthorised access to her data. [2]

(b) Describe the problems that could result if Amber's tablet is hacked. [3]

(a) Amber could use two-factor authentication by sending a code to her mobile phone which has to be typed on the tablet to gain access[1], use biometrics such as face or fingerprint recognition to log in[1], limit the attempts allowed to log in before being locked out[1], create a strong PIN or password[1], avoid leaving the tablet unattended / keep it locked in a drawer overnight so that others cannot physically access it[1], avoid connecting to unsecure Wi-Fi networks[1].

(b) Amber's data may be stolen[1] and then passed on to criminal third parties[1]. This may break the Data Protection Act 2018 regarding appropriate security[1], her employment may be affected[1], her files may be changed or deleted[1], or she may be locked out of her own tablet[1]. Data may be leaked to the public or newspapers[1], or the organisation she works for could be held to ransom[1].

EXAMINATION PRACTICE

1. (a) Describe what is meant by a social engineering attack. [2]
   (b) Describe **one** way in which such an attack may be carried out. [2]
   (c) Describe **two** ways in which a user may protect themselves from a becoming a victim of a successful attack. [4]

2. A bank holds data on a database kept on the organisation's server about each of its account holders, including personal data, credit rating, credit limit and current balance.

   A denial of service attack has been carried out by a disgruntled former employee.
   (a) Explain what is meant by a denial of service attack. [2]
   (b) Describe **one** possible consequence of such an attack on each of
      (i) The bank's customers [2]
      (ii) The bank [2]

3. Sylvia runs a small accounting business from home. She keeps details of all her customers on her desktop computer.
   Describe **two** ways in which this data may be put at risk and suggest a way of reducing the risk in each case. [4]

4. Amy works for a firm of lawyers. She has been warned that confidential client details could be stolen by means of a 'brute force' attack.
   (a) Explain what is meant by 'brute force' in this context. [2]
   (b) Describe **one** way in which a brute force attack can be prevented. [2]

5. Hall Lane School is concerned with protecting its data from external attack.
   (a) A firewall is installed on its computer network. Explain the purpose of a 'firewall' and the principles of how it works. [3]
   (b) Give **two** rules that should be applied to passwords chosen by staff and students accessing the system to reduce the risk of a hacking attack. [2]
   (c) Describe **one** other measure that the school can take to reduce the risk of a malware attack. [2]

6. A network manager is carrying out a penetration test.
   (a) Explain the purpose of penetration testing. [2]
   (b) Describe the principles of how an internal penetration test is carried out. [3]

OPERATING SYSTEMS

The operating system is a group of programs that is essential for managing the computer's resources.

Common examples of operating systems include Windows®, MacOS®, iOS® and Linux®. An Operating System (OS) has five major functions:

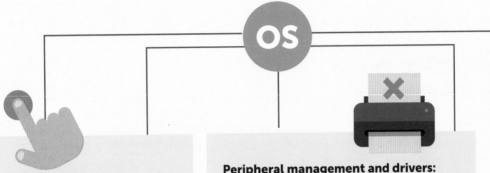

User interface:

The OS provides a means of interacting with the computer, often through buttons, keyboards or mice. An interface may be purely text using a command line interface, menu driven, or a Graphical User Interface (GUI) / WIMP interface e.g. Windows. WIMP stands for Windows, Icons, Menus and Pointer.

Peripheral management and drivers:

Peripheral devices connected externally to the CPU include printers, keyboards and monitors. Users must communicate with devices via the OS. "Out of paper" messages for example, must come via the OS. A buffer is used to compensate for the difference in speed between the CPU and the device.

File management:

The OS allows users to create, delete, move, save and copy files, or allocate them to folders. It can search for files, restore deleted files, free up space for new files and prevent conflicts when two users attempt to modify the same file at once. Access rights to individual files may also be managed.

Memory management and multitasking:

Files and programs need to be in memory for the CPU to perform tasks on them. The OS moves programs and files in and out of memory (from the hard drive or from virtual memory) to process tasks as required. Switching quickly between tasks is known as multi-tasking.

User management:

Different users will each be provided with an account with their own user name and password. Each user can be granted different levels of access depending on their needs and levels of security. The OS can also monitor login activity and log out users after set periods of inactivity.

UTILITY SOFTWARE

Utility programs are small programs that are used in conjunction with the main operating system in order to manage extra features or functions. They are not essential to the running of a computer but make specific tasks easier or add an additional layer of housekeeping.

Three common examples of utility program are:

Defragmentation software

Files are stored on the hard disk in blocks. As different sized files are added and deleted over time, gaps appear which may not fit all of the next file to be stored. Files therefore become fragmented in order to fit them in. Eventually a good clean and tidy up is required that moves everything around to avoid fragmented files. A file saved in three fragments would take three times as long to find it all, so this process speeds up the computer's file retrieval and storage times.

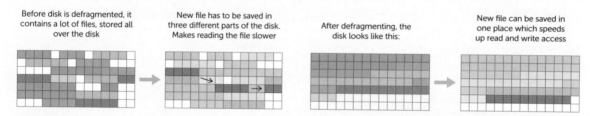

Before disk is defragmented, it contains a lot of files, stored all over the disk

New file has to be saved in three different parts of the disk. Makes reading the file slower

After defragmenting, the disk looks like this:

New file can be saved in one place which speeds up read and write access

Encryption software

Encryption utilities are used to encrypt or decrypt files or folders held on a computer, transmitted across a network or when they are transferred to external devices such as a USB key. The encryption process uses an algorithm and a key to transform plaintext into ciphertext. To decode the original information (the plaintext), it would be necessary to know both the algorithm and the key.

Data compression software

Compression software such as WinZip uses an algorithm to resave the data in an existing file using less space than the original. Sometimes data is lost (lossy compression) and in other times, the file can still be reconstructed without any loss of information (lossless compression).

Compression software is a type of utility program.

(a) Explain **one** situation in which compression software would be useful. [2]

(b) Give **two** other examples of utility software. [2]

(a) When emailing files, compression software enables larger files to fit within email attachment limits[1], it reduces the data transfer volumes to meet ISP limits[1] and saves space on a local disk[1]. Compression software also allows multiple original files to be saved as one single file[1] which is helpful for email and distribution[1].

(b) Encryption software[1], defragmentation software[1], backup utilities[1], anti-virus or anti-spyware software[1], software firewalls[1], auto-update utilities[1] and disk formatting software[1].

EXAMINATION PRACTICE

1. (a) Describe what is meant by multitasking in a computer. [3]
   (b) Memory management is one of the functions of an operating system.
      Describe how memory management enables multitasking to be implemented. [3]

2. List **four** features of an operating system's file management system. [4]

3. Below is a list of five tasks performed by a computer network's operating system:
   A Manages connections with devices using device drivers
   B Allocating access rights to individual users of the network
   C Enabling 'drag and drop' operations
   D Creating a new folder in which to save a spreadsheet
   E Enabling the user to have several applications open and switch between them

   Fill in the right hand side of the table to indicate which part of the operating system is
   responsible for each task. [5]

	A, B, C, D or E
User interface	
Memory management and multitasking	
Peripheral management and drivers	
User management	
File management	

4. Hardeep's computer is taking more time than usual to open and save files after a lot of heavy use.
   Hardeep believes that the disk may have become fragmented.
   (a) Define what Hardeep means when he says the disk has become fragmented. [1]
   (b) Explain how a disk defragmentation utility can help to speed up the computer again if this
      is the case. [2]

5. An operating system is responsible for providing a user interface. Two common interfaces are a
   menu driven interface or a graphical user interface (GUI).
   (a) For each of the scenarios below, tick the type of interface that would be most appropriate. [2]

	Menu-driven interface	Graphical user interface
A smartphone		
An ATM / Bank machine		

   (b) Give **two** advantages of a GUI over a menu-driven interface. [2]

6. A hospital website uses encryption to secure data across network connections.
   Explain the principles of encryption. [3]

ETHICAL, LEGAL, CULTURAL AND ENVIRONMENTAL IMPACT

Every advancement or implementation of a technology may introduce new **ethical, legal, cultural, environmental** and **privacy** issues. These include:

Ethical

AI and machine learning are being developed to recognise faces and behaviour using CCTV in public areas. This software can be used to discriminate against one person over another, or to monitor or restrict access to buildings or highly populated areas based on an individual's criminal record and their behaviour.

Is it right for a computer to discriminate on behaviour? Companies argue that to get such systems right, they need fine tuning which can only happen when a product begins use in practice. At what point is such software 'good enough' to begin using and affecting real people?

Legal

Evidence in legal cases is increasingly being gathered from social networking sites including photos and video, text, location information and relationship details. Given the ease with which 'hackers' can gain access to social networking profiles, the authentication of social media evidence requires checking when, where and how the evidence was collected, the types of evidence and who handled it before it was collected.

Some content on social media sites is illegal, but is the law adequate to prevent dangerous content?

Cultural

Given the ease with which we can access our smartphones, there is growing evidence that the 'always on' culture is increasing our stress levels. The 'Google generation' who have grown up with technology have little to compare against, but our connectivity now means many people spend more time consuming media than sleeping. Managing the balance is key to our well-being.

Do you feel the need to read or respond to a social media post immediately?

Should employees be expected to respond to emails outside of office hours? Do you spend too much time on social media? Are you aware of bullying and trolling on social media?

Environmental

Online shopping has become so easy that some people now use it for up to half of their needs. However, its simplicity has meant that we increasingly use it to buy single items expecting delivery tomorrow.

Is the technology that allows this increasing the miles of polluting delivery vans, or are the routing algorithms now so efficient that home deliveries are in fact better for the environment than people using their own cars? Should there be a minimum order quantity imposed? Is the ease with which we can shop encouraging unnecessary purchases or fuelling unnecessary manufacturing?

Privacy

It has been said that in only a few years, Google will have enough information and capabilities to track the movement of almost everyone who has ever interacted with a Google product. This is based on their daily interactions with others and the websites they visit.

Does this represent a loss of our personal privacy? Who sees this data about us? Should more be done to regulate their data collection or do we accept this as a cost of the services provided?

Ethical and cultural issues

Ethical and cultural issues stemming from the use of computers and digital devices include:

- Providing a means of access to inappropriate or illegal content
- Safety decisions and judgements made by machines, for example self-driving vehicles
- Social platforms or media that enable cyberbullying, trolling or sexting
- Social pressure to be online and purchase more of the latest technology
- Not everyone can pay for digital devices or access broadband Internet. This leads to a 'digital divide'.
- The 'always on' culture and an increase in the reliance on computers in the workplace is leading to an increase in eyestrain and RSI (Repetitive Strain Injury) from prolonged use of screens and keyboards.
- The 'right' level of censorship and monitoring of computer usage and viewable content. These decisions may be made by parents, companies or by entire nations.

Legal issues

There are many legal issues that need to be considered when using computers including:

- How to keep personal data safe.
- How to protect computers from hackers.
- The ability to protect digital media from being illegally copied.

Privacy issues

Concerns surrounding privacy include:

- The ability of websites to track users using their IP address.
- Social media activity and information being used for things we didn't consider at the time of use.
- Threats such as viruses, phishing and pharming can be used to acquire personal data without authority.

Environmental issues

Our use of electronic devices can harm the environment.

- An increase in e-waste and excessive landfill in the UK and abroad, which can in turn leach toxins into the ground, water or air.
- A growing need for rare earth metals and resources causes scarring to the land through mining. Mining also requires significant energy to extract materials.
- Planned obsolescence by manufacturers means that devices have an intentionally limited lifespan before they need to be replaced.

K9Track is a new device designed to be attached to a dog collar. It allows the owner to track the pet's location on a connected smartphone and to monitor the animal's health and levels of exercise each day.

Discuss the ethical, legal and privacy issues that should be considered when creating tracking and monitoring technology such as K9Track. [6]

Since a dog is commonly with their owner, such a tracking device will also be effectively tracking and recording the movements of the (various) owners.[✓] The use of this data will need to be securely stored by the app or cloud service provider.[✓]

The costs of pet insurance or veterinary bills may reduce if its health and movement is monitored and regularly checked.[✓] This may benefit those who can afford the high cost of new devices[✓], widening the digital divide between those who can and cannot afford technology[✓].

The algorithms used to determine what levels of exercise are healthy and what are not for each individual pet will need to be very accurate[✓], taking into prior account an animal's size, weight, breed and general health[✓]. Inaccuracies could lead to blame if an animal's lack of exercise were to blame for ill health[✓].

Monitoring and tracking your pet's movements provides another reason to check your smartphone[✓], increasing the amount of (unnecessary) time spent using technology and looking at screens[✓]. This may negatively impact or reduce the time spent with the pet or family.[✓]

The security of the data[✓] gathered, both accessible through the mobile app and in its raw form stored by the manufacturer will need to be carefully protected from unauthorised access[✓]. A biometric access key[✓] could be used to access the mobile phone app, and the stored data should be adequately protected[✓] (under the Data Protection Act) from malware[✓], hackers[✓] (unauthorised access), social engineering[✓] and interception[✓].

Marks are indicative only. Refer to the band descriptions and levels of response guidance for extended response questions on page 94.

This essay style question is assessed against the levels of response guidelines on page 94. The quality of written communication, including spelling, punctuation and grammar may also be assessed through your response to similar questions.

LEGISLATION

There are four main areas of **legislation** that need to be understood:

- The Data Protection Act 2018
- Computer Misuse Act 1990
- Copyright, Designs and Patents Act 1988
- Software licences (i.e. open source and proprietary)

Data Protection Act 2018

The **Data Protection Act** was updated in 2018 to incorporate the General Data Protection Regulations (GDPR). It has six principles that govern how data should be stored and processed.

These state that data must be:

1. Fairly and lawfully processed
2. Used for specific purposes only
3. Adequate, relevant and not excessive
4. Accurate and up-to-date
5. Not be kept longer than necessary
6. Kept secure

In addition, the data must be kept in accordance with the rights of data subjects.

Computer Misuse Act 1990

The **Computer Misuse Act** was introduced in 1990 to make unauthorised access to programs or data (hacking) and cybercrime illegal. The act recognises three offences:

1. Unauthorised access to computer material.
2. Unauthorised access with intent to commit or facilitate a crime.
3. Unauthorised modification of computer material. It is also illegal to make, supply or obtain anything which can be used in computer misuse offences, including the production and distribution of malware.

Copyright, Designs and Patents Act 1988

This act is designed to protect the works of companies and individuals from being illegally used, copied or distributed. 'Works' include books, music, images, video and software.

SOFTWARE LICENSING

A **software licence** is a contract between the user and the developer or owner that grants permission to use software under given conditions. These conditions may stipulate a time period or further limitations such as non-commercial use only.

Open source software is licenced but free to use. The source code can be viewed and edited. Any derivatives of the work must also be made available (open) to others with the source code.

Proprietary software is created and sold by companies in the form of a licence. You do not own the software or its copyright, only a licence to use it. You will not get access to the source code to modify the software and licences are commonly limited by the number of users. Microsoft Office® is one such example of proprietary software available off-the-shelf.

Freeware is free, but will require a licence, commonly restricting its use and distribution, much like proprietary software.

1. Damon is developing a piece of software to help university students with important timetable reminders.

   He is considering using either an open source or proprietary licence to distribute the software.

   (a) Discuss the advantages and disadvantages of each licence for Damon. [4]

   (b) Damon distributes his software with a proprietary licence. Several students make copies of the software purchased by another student. State which law has been broken. [1]

2. A utility company collects personal data about customers as well as their electricity usage data each month.

   (a) State which piece of legislation covers the security of personal data. [1]

   (b) Give **two** security measures the utility company should put in place in order to provide adequate security of customer data. [2]

1. (a) *Under a proprietary licence, Damon is able to charge for his software[1] and his source code remains hidden[1] meaning that no one can edit or see how it works[1].*

   Damon may not wish to/be able to sell his software for much[1]. Therefore, he may consider a free, open source licence in order to help as many students as he can[1]. He will not get any income from the software[1], but it may help gain traction and reputation for his work[1] which would build a greater number of users[1], and he may be able to profit from advertising[1]. Other programmers may be able to improve his software too[1], but the open source approach may mean Damon loses overall control[1] over his source code and distribution[1].

   (b) Copyright, Designs and Patents Act.[1]

2. (a) *Data Protection Act.[1] (Data must be kept adequately secure.)*

   (b) Firewall[1], anti-virus software[1], passwords[1] or encryption[1].

EXAMINATION PRACTICE

1. Businesses commonly have a policy of replacing their computer hardware and equipment every three years.

   Discuss the environmental impacts of replacing working hardware and equipment so regularly.   [6]

2. James is developing a new software app. He finds some code online which has already been written to solve the same problem.

   (a) Discuss the ethical and legal implications of copying and reusing this code.   [4]

   Once written, James can release the software under a proprietary or open source licence.

   (b) Compare proprietary and open source licensing.   [4]

   (c) Explain **one** advantage to James of releasing the software under a free, open source licence.   [2]

3. Study Table 1 below. For each of the actions, tick the most applicable piece of legislation.   [5]

Action	The Data Protection Act 2018	Computer Misuse Act 1990	Copyright Designs and Patents Act 1988
Using an unlicensed image on a new music album cover for sale			
Collecting and selling customer details to third party companies without their knowledge or permission			
Guessing someone's smartphone PIN to access their messages without their permission			
Failure to change customer details once informed they are inaccurate			
Unauthorised access and modification of company financial accounts			

TOPICS FOR PAPER 2
Computational thinking, algorithms and programming (J277/02)

Information about Paper 2

Written paper: 1 hour and 30 minutes

50% of total GCSE

80 marks

This is a non-calculator paper.

This paper consists of two sections. Students must answer all questions from Section A and Section B.

In Section B, questions assessing students' ability to write or refine algorithms must be answered using either the OCR Exam Reference Language or the high-level programming language they are familiar with.

COMPUTATIONAL THINKING

Principles of computational thinking

Computational thinking is a process used to solve complex problems. It means formulating a problem and expressing its solution in such a way that a computer can carry it out.

There are three basic steps:

- **Abstraction** involves identifying the key parts of the problem and hiding those that aren't important so that it becomes easier to solve. For example, if a program is to be written to simulate a card game, the first task to be accomplished may be 'Shuffle the cards'. This is an abstraction – implementing it will involve specifying a way to randomise 52 variables representing the cards. We can refer to 'shuffle' throughout the program without specifying how it will be done.

- **Decomposition** means breaking down a complex problem into smaller, manageable parts which are easier to solve. This comprises the following steps:

  o Identify the main problem

  o List the main components, functions or tasks

  o Break these down into smaller components or sub-tasks which can then be completed separately. For example:

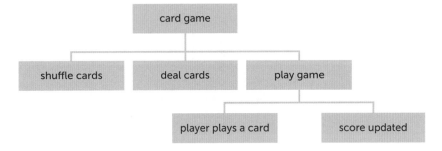

- **Algorithmic thinking** is the consideration that goes into how to solve a problem using one or more algorithms. For instance, there may be two ways to shuffle the cards, but one may make them more random whilst another may be faster. An **algorithm** is the series of steps that a program needs to perform to solve the problem.

A self-driving car is being developed. The software has to be capable of distinguishing between an animal and a person crossing the road in front of it.

(a) Define what is meant by **abstraction**.   [2]

(b) Give **one** example of how abstraction could be used in developing this software.   [1]

(a) *Filtering out/removing/hiding details of a problem[1] that are not relevant to a solution[1].*

(b) *Any example of something that can be removed or hidden, e.g. speed of movement[1], location at which something is crossing[1] / whether it is on a pedestrian crossing[1] / aerodynamic design of the vehicle[1].*

IDENTIFYING THE INPUTS, PROCESSES AND OUTPUTS FOR A PROBLEM

Every problem to be solved using a computer involves input, processing and output.

- The **input** may be entered by someone at a keyboard, it may be a reading from a sensor such as a moisture, pressure or temperature sensor, or another form of input.
- The data then has to be **processed** in some way – for example sorting a list, performing calculations or using temperature readings to predict ice on the roads.
- **Output** is the end result after processing. This could be a printed report, a valve that is opened or closed, or graphics displayed on a screen.

Identify the inputs, processing and outputs in each of these scenarios:

(a) River levels are regularly checked by the Environment Agency and sluice gates opened or closed automatically to control the flow of water. [3]

(b) A utility company emails monthly gas bills to customers. [3]

(c) Exam results for a group of students are entered and validated. A list of names and their results is printed in alphabetical order. [3]

(a) Input: River levels at key points[1]. Processing: Level compared with max and min permissible levels held in system[1]. Output: actuator (or motor) opens or closes sluice gates[1].

(b) Input: customer details[1], meter reading[1], current balance[1]. Processing: calculation of units used[1] and balance due[1]. Output: email to customers showing units used[1], amount due[1].

(c) Input: Exam results[1], student names[1]. Processing: Validation of results[1], sorting of names[1]. Output: error messages[1] (on a display), printed list of results[1].

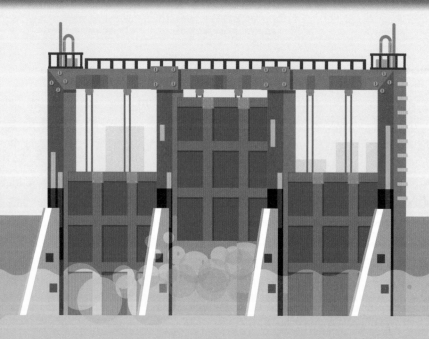

STRUCTURE DIAGRAMS

Identifying inputs, processing and outputs may be the first stage in the **decomposition** of a problem. Each of these stages may then be further broken down. A **structure diagram** may be used to show the structure of a problem, its subsections and links to other subsections.

Example: Library users may use computer terminals to borrow or return a book. Draw a structure diagram to show how this system could work.

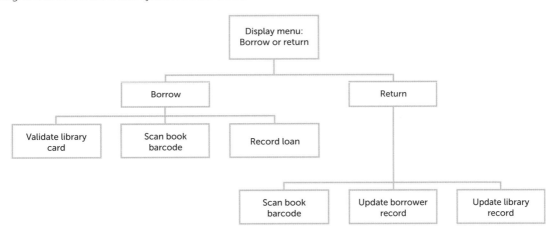

Modules (sections) can be further broken down into subsections. For example, 'Record loan' could have further subsections showing what is involved to carry out this action.

A program is to be written to record new customer details for an online store. A new customer registering for an account enters their name, address and email address, and is given a unique username by the system. They then enter a password, which is validated and must contain a mixture of upper- and lowercase letters and numbers. Once a valid password is entered, it is encrypted and stored with the username and personal details on a permanent storage device.

(a) Describe how **abstraction** could be used in the initial design of the program. [2]

(b) Draw a structure diagram to show how program modules relate to each other. [4]

(a) *The detail of what personal information the user has to enter[1], how the password is validated[1], what happens when an invalid password is entered[1], the encryption algorithm used[1] and where the data is stored[1] can all be ignored at this stage[1].*

(b) *[1 mark for each row of subsections. 1 mark for all subsections connected.]*

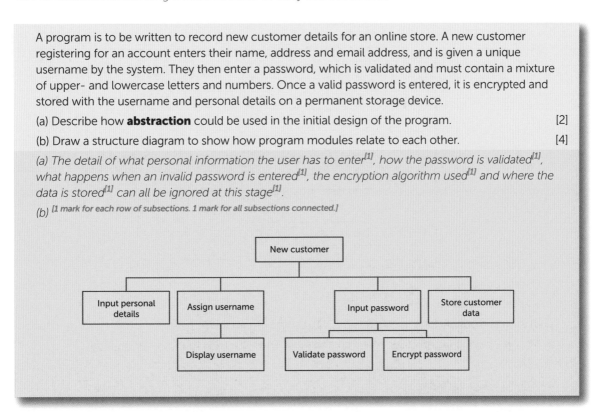

2.1.2

USING FLOWCHARTS

Flowcharts are a useful tool that can be used to develop solutions to a problem. Standard flowchart symbols are shown below:

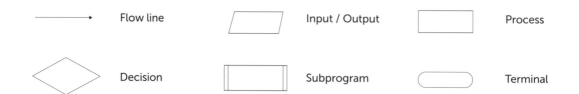

Problem: Draw a flowchart for a program which will count in steps from a start number up to an end number. The user enters the start and end numbers and the step to count in. For example, if the user enters 2, 21, 3, the program will output the numbers 2, 5, 8, 11, 14, 17, 20.

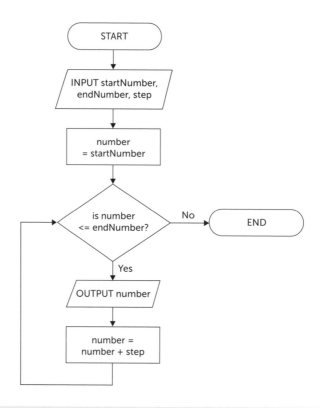

Look at the flowchart above.

(a) What will be output if the user enters 7, 50, 10 for the three values? [1]

(b) What will be output if the user enters an end number which is less than the start number? [1]

(a) 7, 17, 27, 37, 47[1]

(b) Nothing will be output.[1]

USING PSEUDOCODE

The problem with using a flowchart to develop an algorithm is that it does not usually translate very easily into program code.

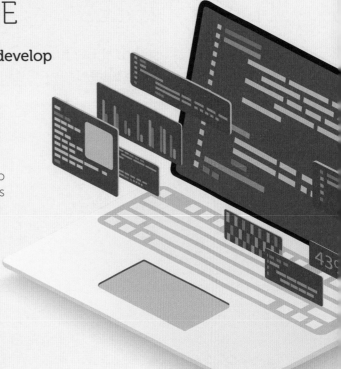

Pseudocode is useful for developing an algorithm using programming-style constructs, but it is not an actual programming language. This means that a programmer can concentrate on figuring out how to solve the problem without worrying about the details of how to write each statement in the programming language that will be used.

Using pseudocode, the algorithm shown in the flowchart above could be expressed like this:

```
input startNumber, endNumber, step
set number to startNumber
while number <= endNumber
    output(number)
    add step to number
endwhile
```

Using OCR Exam Reference Language

OCR has published a formally defined language called **OCR Exam Reference Language** (**ERL**). This is defined in the specification for GCSE Computer Science J277, downloadable from the OCR website.

Some questions in the exam specify that you must use **either** OCR Exam Reference Language **or** a high-level programming language that you have studied to write or complete a program. **Marks are awarded for correctly using syntax to represent programming constructs, whichever language you use**.

The code for the above problem written using OCR Exam Reference Language looks like this:

```
startNumber = input("Enter start number: ")
endNumber = input("Enter end number: ")
step = input("Enter step: ")
number = startNumber
while number <= endNumber
    print(number)
    number = number + step
endwhile
```

Note that if there are three values to be input, you MUST use three input statements if you are asked to use OCR ERL or a programming language rather than pseudocode. Each input statement is used to input a single value and assign it to a variable.

The syntax used in OCR Exam Reference Language (ERL) is explained in more detail in Section 8.

TRACE TABLES

A trace table is used to show how the values of variables change during execution of a program.

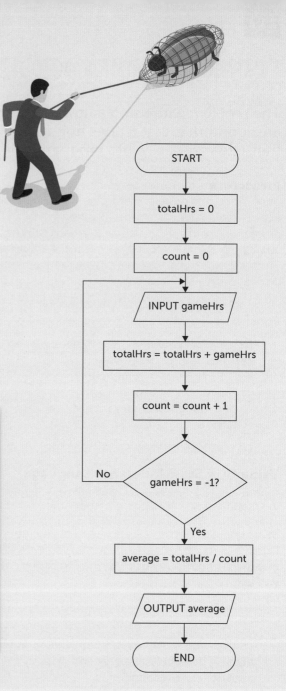

As each line of code is executed, the current value of any variable or logical expression that is changed is written in the appropriate column of the table. It is not necessary to fill in a cell if the value has not changed from the line above.

Example: Ben designs a flowchart for an algorithm to calculate the average number of hours students spend per week playing computer games. He uses test data for 3 students spending respectively 8, 10 and 12 hours playing games. This should result in an average of 10 hours.

1. The flowchart opposite contains an error. Describe how the algorithm could be corrected. [3]

The input, gameHrs, should be tested right after it has been input.[1] However, a program cannot jump out of a loop before completing it.[1] Therefore, the input statement and the test for gameHrs = −1 should be placed at the end of the loop.[1] An initial input statement is required before entering the loop.[1]

Download the Python program solution from **www.clearrevise.com**

gameHrs	totalHrs	count	gameHrs = −1?	average
	0	0		
8	8	1	No	
10	18	2	No	
12	30	3	No	
−1	29	4	Yes	7.25

Oops! The algorithm must be incorrect, since it produces the wrong answer.

Identifying common errors

There are two types of error that can occur in program code. A **syntax error** occurs when a statement is written which does not obey the rules of the programming language. Common syntax errors include:

- writing a single statement to input two variables:

```
input("Please enter x and y", x, y)      - is incorrect. It should be:
x = input("Please input x ")
y = input("Please enter y ")
```

- writing output statements incorrectly:

```
print(Total sum = , totalSum)            - should be written:
print("Total sum = ", totalSum)          - don't forget the quote marks!
```

- writing Boolean conditions incorrectly:

```
if x < 1 OR > 100                         - should be written:
if x < 1 OR x > 100
```

A **logic error** occurs when the program does not do what the user intended or gives an answer that isn't what the programmer intended.

If you do any programming you will likely discover many ways of making logic errors.

2. The code below should add all even numbers between 1 and 50.

```
count = 0
while count <= 50:
    count = count + 2
    sum = sum + count
print(Total:, sum)
```

Find **two** errors in this code. State in each case whether they are logic errors or syntax errors.   [4]

sum has not been initialised.[1] This is a logic error[1].
count <= 50 will cause the number 52 to be included, as the while condition is not checked until all the statements in the loop have been executed. Two statements within the while loop should be swapped.[1] Logic error.[1] print(Total:, *sum) doesn't have the string in quote marks.[1] It should be:* print("Total:", sum)[1]. *Syntax error.[1]*

SEARCHING ALGORITHMS

Binary search

A binary search can be used to search a list that is in numerical or alphabetical order. It works by repeatedly dividing in half the portion of the list that could contain the required data item.

Example: An ordered list of 12 numbers contains the following data items. To find whether the number 37 is in the list, start by examining the middle item in the list (this is the sixth item in this list of 12 numbers.)

25	26	28	37	39	40	41	43	56	70	74	81

Stage 1: The search item 37 is less than 40. Discard all the items greater than or equal to 40.

25	26	28	37	39

Stage 2: The middle item is the third item, which is 28. 37 is greater than 28, so discard items less than or equal to 28.

37	39

Stage 3: The 'middle' item in a list of two numbers is the first one 37. This is the number we are searching for, so the algorithm can report that the number has been found. If we had been searching for, say, 36, we would know at this stage that the number is not in the list.

37

Sometimes the search item is found before completing all stages. If we had been searching for the number 40, we would have found it at Stage 1, its position in the list would be returned and the algorithm could then be made to terminate.

Linear search

In a linear search each item will be checked one by one in the list. This is very slow for large lists, but necessary if the list is not sorted. For large, sorted lists, a binary search is much more efficient as the number of items to be examined is halved at each stage. Using a binary search, only a maximum of 20 items will have to be examined to determine whether an item is present in a list of a million items.

A list of names is shown below.

Anne	Bob	Chas	Eric	Fiona	Harry	Jo	Ken	Mona	Nahim	Geri	Peter	Steve	Zoe

(a) State which items are examined when looking for **Steve** using a binary search. [2]

(b) State which items are examined when looking for **Dave** using a binary search. [4]

(c) State how many items will be examined when looking for **Dave** in the list of names using a linear search. [1]

(a) Jo[1], Geri[1], (Steve will be the next search item).

(b) Jo[1], Chas[1], Fiona[1], Eric[1], (name not found).

(c) 14[1]

BUBBLE SORT

A bubble sort works by repeatedly going through the list to be sorted, swapping adjacent elements if they are in the wrong order.

To sort a list of n items, a maximum of n−1 passes is required. (The items may be alphabetical or numeric.)

Example

A list of 5 numbers 7, 3, 5, 9, 4 is to be sorted. Show the state of the list after each pass.

List

7	3	5	9	4

Pass 1

3	7	5	9	4
3	5	7	9	4
3	5	7	9	4
3	5	7	4	9

Examine 5 items

After the first pass through the list, the largest number has 'bubbled' to the end of the list. In the second pass, we only need to compare the first four items.

Pass 2

3	5	7	4	9
3	5	7	4	9
3	5	4	7	9

Examine 4 items

Pass 3

3	5	4	7	9
3	4	5	7	9

Examine 3 items

Pass 4

3	4	5	7	9

Examine 2 items

The list is now sorted.

The list of animals **hamster, rabbit, dog, cat, goldfish**, is to be sorted in alphabetical order using a bubble sort.

Show the state of the list after:

(a) Pass 1   [1]

(b) Pass 2   [1]

   (a) hamster, dog, cat, goldfish, rabbit[1]

   (b) dog, cat, goldfish, hamster, rabbit[1]

The bubble sort algorithm is not efficient for large lists. Note that in some cases, the algorithm may have sorted the list before performing the full number of passes. If no swaps are made during a particular pass, then the list must already be sorted. This condition could be tested and the algorithm could be made to terminate.

The algorithm for the bubble sort, including this modification, is given on page 58.

MERGE SORT

This is a very fast two-stage sort. In the first stage, the list is successively divided in half, forming two sublists, until each sublist is of length one.

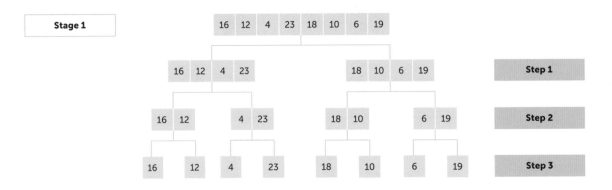

At the end of stage 1, all the elements have been separated out.

In the second stage, each pair of sublists is repeatedly merged to produce new sorted sublists until there is only one sublist remaining. This is the sorted list.

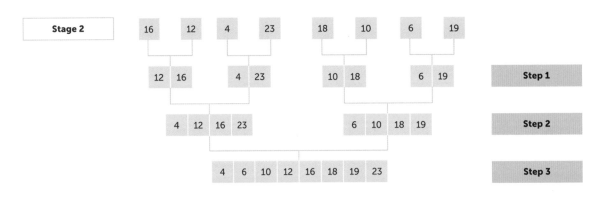

1. Write the list that results from merging the two lists 2, 5, 17, 38, 56 and 3, 4, 15,19, 36   [1]

2. The following list is to be sorted using a merge sort algorithm.

Giraffe	Zebra	Monkey	Leopard	Hippo	Warthog	Rhino

(a) Describe the two stages of a merge sort algorithm.   [4]

(b) Write out the list after Step 2 of the Stage 2 process.   [2]

1. *The list would be: 2, 3, 4, 5, 15, 17, 19, 36, 38, 56[1]*

2. *(a) Stage 1: The list is successively divided in half[1], forming two sublists[1], until each sublist is of length one[1].*
   Stage 2: Each pair of sublists[1] is repeatedly merged[1] to produce new sorted sublists[1] until there is only one sublist remaining[1].
   (b) Giraffe, Leopard, Monkey, Zebra,[1]   Hippo, Rhino, Warthog[1]

INSERTION SORT

This algorithm is more efficient than the bubble sort. Starting with the second item in the list, it looks at each remaining item and places it in the correct position in the list. (This is similar to how you might sort a deck of cards.)

Example: Sort the list **Philip**, **Max**, **Keira**, **Vic**, **Sara**, **Jan** into alphabetical order using an insertion sort.

List	Phillip	Max	Keira	Vic	Sara	Jan
Pass 1	Max	Phillip	Keira	Vic	Sara	Jan
Pass 2	Keira	Max	Phillip	Vic	Sara	Jan
Pass 3	Keira	Max	Phillip	Vic	Sara	Jan
Pass 4	Keira	Max	Phillip	Sara	Vic	Jan
Pass 5	Jan	Keira	Max	Phillip	Sara	Vic

The following list of numbers is to be sorted using an insertion sort:

16	12	4	23	18	10

(a) Show the state of the list after the first number is moved. [1]

(b) Show the state of the list after the second number is moved. [1]

(c) How many numbers have to be moved altogether before the list is sorted? Explain your answer. [4]

(d) Explain **one** reason why a programmer may decide to use a merge sort rather than a bubble sort or an insertion sort when a list of items needs to be sorted. [2]

(a)

12	16	4	23	18	10	[1]

(b)

4	12	16	23	18	10	[1]

(c) *Four numbers are moved.[1] First number examined is 12, which is moved to the front of the list. [1] The second number is examined is 4, and this is moved to the front of the list.[1] The third number examined is 23, and this is not moved as it is in the correct position.[1] 18 is examined and moved to between 16 and 23.[1] 10 is moved between 4 and 12.[1]*

(d) *When the list contains a very large number of items[1], a merge sort will execute many times faster than a bubble sort or an insertion sort[1]. This is even more important when the list is regularly amended and needs to be re-sorted each time.[1] (Tip: An answer "Because it is faster" will only get one of the two marks. You need to mention the size of the list – the difference in execution time is not significant for a list of say 100 items, but for 100,000 it is significant.)*

IDENTIFYING ALGORITHMS

Bubble sort

```
//Bubble sort
array aList = [17, 3, 7, 15, 13, 23, 20]
//get number of items in the array
numItems = aList.length
passNumber = numItems - 1
swapMade = True
while passNumber > 0 AND swapMade
    swapMade = False
    for j = 0 to passNumber - 1
        if aList[j] > aList[j + 1] then
            temp = aList[j]
            aList[j] = aList[j + 1]
            aList[j + 1] = temp
            swapMade = True
        endif
    next j
    passNumber = passNumber - 1
endwhile
print("Sorted list: ", aList)
```

Insertion sort

```
//Insertion sort
array aList = [17, 3, 7, 15, 13, 23, 20]
listLength = aList.length
for index = 1 to listLength -1
    current = aList[index]
    pos = index
    while pos > 0 AND aList[pos-1] > current
        aList[pos] = aList[pos - 1]
        pos = pos - 1
    endwhile
    aList[pos] = current
next index
print("Sorted list: ", aList)
```

Linear search

```
//Linear search
array aList[10]
aList = [14, 2, 3, 11, 1, 9, 5, 8, 10, 6]
print("List to be searched: ", aList)
found = False
index = 0
searchItem = int(input("Number sought: "))
while NOT found AND index < aList.length
    if aList[index] == searchItem then
        found = True
    else
        index = index + 1
    endif
endwhile
if found then
    print(searchItem, "found in position",
    index, " of the list.")
else
    print("Item not found")
endif
```

Binary search

```
//Binary search
array aList[10]
aList = [2, 3, 11, 12, 15, 19, 23, 30, 36, 45]
print("List to be searched: ", aList)
found = False
first = 0
last = aList.length - 1
searchItem = int(input("Number sought: "))
while NOT found AND first <= last
    midpt = int((first + last) / 2)
    if aList[midpt] == searchItem then
        found = True
        index = midpt
    else
    if aList[midpt] < searchItem then
        first = midpt + 1
    else
        last = midpt - 1
    endif
endwhile
if found
    print("Found at position ", index,
          " in the list.")
else
    print("Item is not in the list.")
endif
```

EXAMINATION PRACTICE

1. An algorithm is given below.

```
01  array aList = [3,6,7,9,13,15,16,19,20,24,26,29,36]
02  found = False
03  n = 0
04  x = input("Enter a number: ")
05  while NOT found AND n < aList.length
06      print(aList[n])
07      if aList[n] == x then
08          found = True
09      else
10          n = n + 1
11      endif
12  endwhile
13  if found then
14      print(x, " found at position ", n)
15  else
16      print("invalid number")
17  endif
```

(a) At line 05, what is the value of **aList.length**? [1]

(b) The user enters 9 at line 04. What is printed at line 06 the first 3 times the
    while...endwhile loop is performed? [3]

(c) State what will be printed at line 14 if the user enters the number 9. [1]

(d) Explain the purpose of this algorithm. [2]

2. An array **names** holds **n** items. An algorithm for a bubble sort is given below.

```
01  swapMade = True
02  while swapMade
03      swapMade = False
04      for index = 0 to n - 2
05          if names[index] > names[index+1] then
06              swap the names
07              swapMade = True
08          endif
09      next index
10  endwhile
```

(a) Explain the purpose of the variable swapMade in the algorithm. [2]

(b) Write the code for "*swap the names*" in line 06. [3]

(c) The list **names** contains the following:

   Edna   Adam   Victor   Charlie   Jack   Ken   Maria

   Write the contents of the list after each of the first two times the **while...endwhile** loop
   is executed. [2]

(d) How many times will the **while** loop be executed before the program terminates?
    Explain your answer. [2]

3. For each of the following activities, state whether they are examples of abstraction, decomposition or algorithmic thinking.

   (a) Planning a series of step-by-step instructions specifying how a computer will solve a problem. [1]

   (b) Identifying the subtasks involved in solving a problem, and further breaking down the subtasks into ones which can be solved more easily. [1]

   (c) Filtering out details of a problem that are not relevant to a solution. [1]

4. An algorithm is given below.

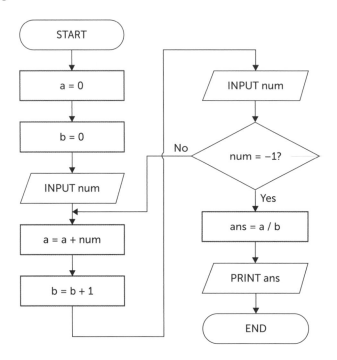

   (a) Complete the trace table to show how the variables change, and what will be output, if the numbers 3, 8, 2, 5, –1 are entered. [4]

   (b) State the purpose of the algorithm. [1]

num	a	b	ans
	0	0	0
3	3	1	0
8			

VARIABLES, CONSTANTS, ASSIGNMENTS

Data used in a program is stored in memory locations while the program is running. A **variable** is a memory location holding a data item which may change value during program execution.

The table below shows the different data types found in programming languages such as Python or VB.

Data type	Type of data	Examples
Integer	A whole number	3, −170, 176500
Real/float	A number with a decimal point	3.142, 78.0, −0.5678
Char/character	A single character or symbol that can be typed	A, #, @, 6, !
String	Zero or more characters enclosed in quote marks	"yes", "Hi John"
Boolean	Can only take the value True or False	True, False

Some programming languages allow the use of **constants**. The value of a constant cannot change during the execution of the program.

```
const VAT = 0.2
```

A **variable name** can be a mixture of letters and numbers, but should start with a letter. Uppercase letters and lowercase letters may be used – note, for example, that the variable name `Total` is treated as different from `total`. The **value** of a variable (not its name) can change during program execution.

CamelCase is commonly used to separate words making up a variable name; for example, `totalCost`, `studentName`. Variable names by convention start with a lowercase letter, and constants are usually written in uppercase and 'snakecase' such as MAX_NUMBER_OF_PLAYERS.

Using a naming convention such as this helps to reduce errors in writing variable names in a program. If no convention has been used, it can be difficult to remember whether, for example, a total cost is named `totalCost`, `totalcost`, `Totalcost`, `total_cost` or something else. It also aids other programmers who may need to update a pre-existing program.

A **variable** is assigned a value using the = sign.

```
costPrice = 15.65
count = count + 3          (This increases the value of the variable  count  by 3)
under12 = True
studentName = "Higgins, P"
```

A game is being programmed.

(a) (i) Choose a meaningful variable name for the highest score in the game. [1]

    (ii) Set the highest score to 25. [1]

(b) (i) Choose a meaningful variable name for the name of a player. [1]

    (ii) Set the player's name to "Santos". [1]

(c) Explain the reason why variable names are commonly written using 'camelCase'. [2]

(a) (i) (ii) highScore[1] = 25[1]   (b) (i) (ii) playerName[1] = "Santos"[1]

(c) So they are consistent[1], easier to remember[1] and therefore reduce programming errors.[1]

INPUTS, OUTPUTS AND OPERATORS

When data needs to be input, the user is typically prompted to type something, and whatever they type is assigned to a variable. The input statement shown below does this in a single line:

```
name = input("Please enter your name: ")
```

1. Write an input statement that asks the user to enter a telephone number. [2]

```
phoneNumber =[1] input("Enter your telephone number: ")[1]
```

The **print** statement is used to output data to the screen.

Example: Write statements which ask the user to enter two numbers for the length and breadth of a rectangle, calculates and prints the area.

```
length = input("Enter length: ")

breadth = input("Enter breadth: ")

area = length * breadth

print("Area = ", area)
```

You will lose marks if you write the input statement as `input(phoneNumber)`. *This is not correct syntax. It would be acceptable to write* `phoneNumber = input()`

You can use the concatenation operator '+' instead of a comma ',' in a print statement, but you cannot mix strings and numbers. Numbers must first be converted to strings:

```
print("Area = " + str(area))
```

Arithmetic and comparison operators

Arithmetic operators	
+	Addition
−	Subtraction
*	Multiplication
/	Division
MOD	Modulus
DIV	Quotient
^	Exponentiation

Comparison operators	
==	Equal to
!=	Not equal to
<	Less than
<=	Less than or equal to
>	Greater than
>=	Greater than or equal to

MOD returns the remainder when one integer is divided by another. For example:

`x = 22 MOD 5` will give the result `x = 2`.

`x = 15 MOD 5` will give the result `x = 0`.

DIV gives the quotient (the result as a whole number without the remainder), so `x = 17 DIV 5` is 3, and `22 DIV 5` is 4.

2. What will these Boolean conditions evaluate to?

(a) "Fred" != "fred" [1]

(b) 1 <= 4 AND 7 <= 7 [1]

(a) *True*[1]

(b) *True*[1]

SEQUENCE AND SELECTION

Sequence

Sequence means statements are written one after the other and execution follows the same order.

To input and print the total of three numbers:

```
num1 = input("Enter first number")
num2 = input("Enter next number")
num3 = input("Enter next number")
total = num1 + num2 + num3
print(total)
```

Selection

Selection statements involve an **if .. then**, **if .. then .. else** or **case** statement.

For example, suppose we wanted to print the largest of the three numbers entered:

```
if num1 >= num2 AND num1 >= num3 then
    print("maximum is ", num1)
elseif num2 >= num1 AND num2 >= num3 then
    print("maximum is ", num2)
else
    print("maximum is ", num3)
endif
```

An algorithm to check a user password has been written in pseudocode. This has been rewritten on the right using the OCR Exam Reference Language (ERL):

Ask user to enter password
input password
If password not = "SP123"
    display "Invalid password"

→

```
password = input("Please enter password: ")
if password != "SP123" then
    print("Invalid password")
endif
```

A **case** statement is a useful selection tool when there are several alternative paths depending on the value of a variable:

```
switch member:
    case "JuniorMember":
        entry = 2.0
    case "SeniorMember":
        entry = 3.0
    default:
        entry = 5.0
endswitch
```

Write a Boolean condition to test whether a variable named `result` is between 1 and 10.   [1]

if result >= 1 AND result <= 10 then...[1]

Note that writing: `if result >= 1 AND <= 10 then...`
is incorrect and will score no marks. If you need the opposite condition you could write: `if NOT(result >= 1 AND result <= 10) then...`

ITERATION

Iteration means repetition. There are three types of iteration statement:

---

for ... next loop

A **for ... next loop**, which is controlled by a count which is automatically incremented each time the loop is performed. An optional 'step' can be used to increment the count by any integer.

```
for count = 1 to 10
    print(count)
next count
```

This will print all the numbers from 1 to 10.

```
for count = 1 to 10 step 2
    print(count)
next count
```

This will print the numbers 1, 3, 5, 7, 9. Note that the step may be positive or negative. So the loop condition could be written as: `for count = 10 to 7 step -1` which would print the numbers 10, 9, 8, 7.

---

1. Complete the following program, which allows the user to enter a start number and an end number, and prints out all the numbers in between which are divisible by either 3 or 7, or both.　　[3]

```
startNum = input("Enter start number")
endNum = input("Enter end number: ")
for count = ........................
    if count MOD 3 == 0 ...................... then
        ......................
next count
```

```
startNum = input("Enter start number")
endNum = input("Enter end number: ")
for count = startNum to endNum[1]
    if count MOD 3 == 0 OR count MOD 7 == 0[1] then
        print(count)[1]
    endif
next count
```

---

while ... endwhile loop

A **while ... endwhile** loop is condition-controlled. The condition is checked before the loop is entered, so in the example below, if **mark** = −1 before entering the **while** loop, none of the statements in the loop will be executed.

```
total = 0
mark = input("Enter first mark: ")
while mark != -1
    total = total + mark
    mark = input("Enter next mark: ")
endwhile
```

do ... until loop

A **do ... until** loop is another condition-controlled loop. The specified condition is tested at the end of the loop, so the loop is always executed at least once.

```
total = 0
mark = 0
do
    total = total + mark
    mark = input("Enter next mark: ")
until mark == -1
```

2. Write a program to allow the user to enter seven daily temperatures, calculate and then print the maximum and minimum temperatures. [5]

```
totalTemp = 0[1]
for count = 1 to 7[1]
    temp = input("Enter temperature: ")[1]
    totalTemp = totalTemp + temp[1]
next count
average = totalTemp / 7[1]
print("Average = ", average)[1]
```

Nested loop

You can have one loop nested inside another.
Example: Display all the multiplication tables between 2 and 10

```
for table = 2 to 10
   for n = 1 to 10
      answer = table * n
      print(table, " x ", n, " = ", answer)
   next n
next table
```

3. There are two loops in the above code.
   How many times will the print statement be executed in the above example?
   Explain your answer. [2]

4. Explain what will happen when the following code snippet is executed: [2]

```
total = 0
x = 0
while x != 100
    total = total + x
    x = x + 3
endwhile
print("total = ", x)
```

3. A for..next loop is a count controlled loop. The print statement is executed 90 times.[1] The outer for...next loop is executed 9 times.[1] Each time the outer for...next loop is executed, the inner loop is executed 10 times.[1]

*4. x will never be 100[1], so the program will result in an **infinite loop**.[1] x = 0, 3, 6,... 99, 102[1]*

DATA TYPES AND CASTING

You have used the data types **integer**, **real** (called **float** in some programming languages), **string** and **Boolean**. The **char** data type holds a single character.

Converting to another data type (casting)

Converting to another data type is called **casting**. A language such as Python accepts all input from the user as a string. Therefore, if the user enters something that should be interpreted as an integer, real or Boolean value, it has to be converted.

Function	Example	Result
`str()`	`x = str(264985)`	`x = "264985"`
`int()`	`x = int("76")`	`x = 76`
`float()`	`x = float("3.75")`	`x = 3.75`
`real()`	`x = real("3.75")`	`x = 3.75`
`bool()`	`x = bool("True")`	`x = True`

Example: Python accepts all inputs as strings. Use Python code to input two integers a and b, add them and output the result c.

```
a = int(input("Enter first integer: "))
b = int(input("Enter second integer: "))
c = a + b
print(c)
```

1. The user enters 2 and 3 in the above example.
   (a) What will be output? [1]
   (b) What will be output if the user writes the first two lines as:
   ```
   a = real(input("Enter first number: "))
   b = real(input("Enter second number: "))
   print(a + b)
   ```
   [1]
   (c) What will be output if the user writes the first two lines as:
   ```
   a = input("Enter first number: ")
   b = input("Enter second number: ")
   ```
   [1]
2. Explain why a telephone number should be entered as a string rather than an integer. [2]

1. (a) 5[1]   (b) 5.0[1]   (c) 23[1] (The + will mean concatenate as the inputs give two strings.)

2. Because it may have a leading 0[1], which will not be displayed[1], or an international code such as +44, or contain spaces and brackets[1], which will cause an error if entered as an integer[1].

STRING MANIPULATION

Concatenating and indexing strings

Concatenating means 'joining together'. So:

```
"Alan" + "Bates" = "AlanBates"
"2" + "3" = "23"
```

Each character in a string can be referenced by its **index**, starting at 0.

Thus, if `studentName = "Jumal"`

then `studentName[0]` will contain `"J"` and `studentName[3]` will contain `"a"`.

Substrings

Using indexing, you can isolate a single character or several characters in a string. For example, if the first three characters of a 9-character product code represent product type, and the next four characters represent the year of manufacture, you can isolate these strings using different **string methods** and string handling operations. Using OCR ERL:

```
productCode = "GAR201834"
productType = productCode.left(3)
year = productcode.subString(3,4)
print("Product type = ", productType)
print("Year = ", year)
```

Note: `productType` and `year` are both string variables. Therefore, you could concatenate them in the print statements and write:

```
print("Product type = " +
      productType)

print("Year = " + year)
```

This will print:

```
Product type = GAR
Year = 2018
```

Write a program which asks the user to enter a firstname and a surname, and outputs the surname followed by a space and the initial letter of the firstname. [4]

```
//Program name: surname and initial
firstname = input("Enter firstname: ")[1]
surname = input("Enter surname: ")[1]
initial = firstname[0][1]
print(surname, initial)[1]      // or print(surname + " " + initial)[1]
```

String methods

To convert a string to upper or lowercase:
```
product = "Garden Hose"
print(product.upper, " ", product.lower)
```

will print: `GARDEN HOSE garden hose`

To convert a character to its ASCII value: `aVal = ASC('A')` will return 65 in `aVal`.
To convert an ASCII value to a character: `aChar = CHR(98)` will return `'b'` in `aChar`.

ARRAYS

An array is a data structure of fixed length used to hold several items of the same data type. An empty array with seven elements can be declared with the statement **array day[7]**. The array could be initialised to contain the names of the days of the week like this:

```
day = ["Sun","Mon","Tues","Wed","Thurs","Fri","Sat"]
```

Items are referred to using their index, or position in the array, starting at 0. Thus the third item (Tues) in this array is referred to as **day[2]**.

Example: Write a program to enter the number of customers visiting a shop each day of the week and then print out the total number of customers for the week.

```
01    array day[7]
02    day = ["Sun","Mon","Tues","Wed","Thurs","Fri","Sat"]
03    array customers[7]                    //define an empty array
04    customers = [0,0,0,0,0,0,0]           //initialise the array
05    totalCustomers = 0
06    for n = 0 to 6
07        print(day[n], ": ")
08        customers[n] = input("Enter number of customers: ")
09        totalCustomers = totalCustomers + customers[n]
10    next n
11    for n = 0 to 6
12        print(day[n], customers[n])
13    next n
14    print("Total customers ", totalCustomers)
```

1. What will be output at line 07 the third time the FOR...NEXT loop is executed? [1]
2. Define an array called **numbers** holding five numbers 37, 76, 55, 91, 23. Write a program to reverse the order of the numbers, storing them in a second array called **reverseNumbers**. Print out the contents of **reverseNumbers**. [5]

1. *Tues:* [1]

2. *array numbers[5]* [1]
   numbers = [37, 76, 55, 91,23] [1]
   array reverseNumbers[5] [1]
   for index = 0 to 4 [1]
       reverseNumbers[index] = numbers[4-index] [1]
   next index [1]
   print("Reverse numbers: ", reverseNumbers) [1]

TWO-DIMENSIONAL ARRAYS

An array may have two or more dimensions. A 2-dimensional array named **sales** could hold the number of properties sold each quarter (Jan–March, April–June, July–September, October–December) by three different branches of an estate agent.

	Index	0	1	2	3
Three branches	0	56	87	92	43
	1	167	206	387	54
	2	22	61	52	14

The index for both row and column of the array starts at 0. The array is defined with the statement `array sales[3,4]`. The number of properties sold in Quarter 4 by Agent 1 is held in `sales[0,3]` and has the value 43.

1. The three branches of the estate agency are known as Branch A, Branch B and Branch C.
   (a) Write code to output the sales figure for Branch C for the period April–June. [1]
   (b) What will be output? [1]
2. Write a program to ask a user to enter the name and five race times in seconds for each of 3 competitors. It should then display the average time for each competitor. [6]

1. (a) $print(sales[2,1])$[1]   (b) 61[1]

2.
```
array name[3]                  [1]
array totalTime[3]
array averageTime[3]
array raceTime[3,5]            [1] Initialise variables
totalTime = [0,0,0]
for c = 0 to 2                 [1]
    name[c] = input("Enter name: ")   [1]
    for r = 0 to 4             [1]
        raceTime[c,r] = int(input("Enter race time: "))   [1]
        totalTime[c] = totalTime[c] + raceTime[c,r]       [1]
    next r                     [1]
    averageTime[c] = totalTime[c] / 5                     [1]
    print("Average raceTime for ", name[c], averageTime[c])   [1]
next c
```

STRUCTURED RECORDS

A **database** is a collection of records each having an identical record structure. Each field in a record has a defined field type such as integer, real, currency, Boolean or string.

VolcanoTable

name	country	lastErupted	explosivityIndex	elevationMetres
Taal	Philippines	2020	4	311
White Island	New Zealand	2019	2	321
Shiveluch	Russia	2019	4	3283
Anak Krakatoa	Indonesia	2018	3	813
Eyjafjallajökull	Iceland	2010	4	2119
Etna	Italy	2013	3	3350
Stromboli	Italy	2019	2	924
Puyehue-Cordón Caulle	Chile	2011	5	2236

Look at the table above.

(a) Write an SQL statement to display the name and last eruption of all volcanoes in Italy. [3]

(b) List the names of all the volcanoes which will be displayed when the query for part (a) is run. [2]

(c) Write an SQL statement to display all the fields for volcanoes in countries whose name begins with the letter "I". [3]

*(a) **SELECT** name, lastErupted[1]*
 *   **FROM** VolcanoTable[1]*
 *   **WHERE** country = 'Italy'[1]*

(b) Etna and Stromboli.[1]

*(c) **SELECT** *[1]*
 *   **FROM** VolcanoTable[1]*
 *   **WHERE** country LIKE 'I%'[1]*

USING SQL TO SEARCH FOR DATA

Records in this format can be searched using a Structured Query Language (SQL).

The format of an SQL statement is:

> **SELECT**... field1, field2, field3...
> **FROM**... table
> **WHERE**... criteria

Using the Volcanoes table above, the SQL statement below will return a Results table showing all eruptions since 2019:

> **SELECT** name, country, lastErupted, explosivityIndex
> **FROM** VolcanoTable
> **WHERE** lastErupted >= '2019'

Results table

name	country	lastErupted	explosivityIndex
White Island	New Zealand	2019	2
Shiveluch	Russia	2019	4
Stromboli	Italy	2019	2

You can also use Boolean operators to search for data. To find the lowest or most significant volcanoes:

> **SELECT** name, country, lastErupted, elevationMetres
> **FROM** VolcanoTable
> **WHERE** explosivityIndex = 5 OR elevationMetres < 500

Results table

name	country	lastErupted	elevationMetres
Taal	Philippines	2020	311
White Island	New Zealand	2019	321
Puyehue-Cordón Caulle	Chile	2011	2236

Wildcards

The wildcard * is a substitute for ALL fields, e.g. SELECT *
The Boolean condition LIKE is used with the wildcard %, which is a substitute for zero or more characters, e.g.

> **WHERE** name **LIKE** 'S%'

finds all records with names beginning with S.

FILE HANDLING OPERATIONS

When data needs to be stored in non-volatile storage such as a hard disk or SSD, it is written to a **file**.

Text files

Text files contain text in lines. Each line of the text file comprises a **record**, and the different **fields** in the record are separated by commas. For example, a file containing the membership number, surname and firstname of club members could look like this when stored in a text file: There are four basic file handling operations: **Open**, **Read**, **Write**, **Close**.

*members - Notepad
File Edit Format View Help
```
234,Harrison,Jane
235,Kitson,Keith
236,Mehmed,Jas
240,Okello,Paul
246,Nelson,Harriet
247,Larsson,Kurt
```

Creating, opening, writing to and closing a new file

The program code for creating a new file and writing to it depends on the language used. In OCR ERL, a new member file could be created, and records written, using the code below:

```
newfile("members.txt")                        //create a new file
memberfile = open("members.txt")              //open the file
member = input("enter member number, surname, firstname
               separated by commas")     //input the first record
while NOT member == "x"
   memberfile.writeLine(member)
   member = input("enter member number, surname,firstname
                  separated by commas")  //if it's "x", exit loop
endwhile
memberfile.close()
```

Note that if the file already exists, the newfile() statement is omitted, and new records will automatically be appended to the end of the file.

Reading and printing all records in a file

```
memberfile = open("members.txt") //open the file
while NOT memberfile.endOfFile()
     print(memberfile.readLine())
endwhile
memberfile.close()               //close the file
```

Separating out the fields is more complex and is not covered in this specification.

Write a program to enter the titles of the 10 most popular films of the previous year and store them in a text file. You need to create and open the file, add the records and then close the file. [5]

```
newfile("films.txt")[1]               //create a new file
filmfile = open("films.txt")[1]    // open the file
for count = 1 to 10[1]
   filmTitle = input("enter film title: ")[1]
   filmFile.writeLine(filmTitle)[1]
next count[1]
filmfile.close()[1]
```

2.2.3

SUBPROGRAMS

There are two types of subprogram, **functions** and **procedures**. Programming languages have many built-in functions such as `input`, `int` and `print`:

`x = input("Enter a number")` displays a prompt and assigns the user input to variable `x`.
`num = int("345")` converts the string `"345"` to an integer and assigns it to variable `num`.

Writing a function

A **function** is written to convert a Celsius temperature to Fahrenheit.

```
function convertToF(Ctemperature)
    Ftemperature = (Ctemperature * 9/5) + 32
    return Ftemperature
endfunction
```

To call the function and assign the Fahrenheit temperature to `tempInF`:

```
celsiusTemp = input("Enter temperature in celsius: ")
tempInF = convertToF(celsiusTemp)
```

Parameters

`Ctemperature` is an example of a **parameter**.

Random number generation

The function `random(a,b)` will return a random number between two integers a and b.

Local and global variables

All variables have a **scope**, which defines the parts of a program in which they are recognised. In the function below, `totalScore`, `throw1` and `throw2` are **local variables**. They are not recognised outside the subroutine and if you try to use them in the main program, you will get an error message. The scope of **a global variable** is the whole program including all its subroutines.

> Write a function throwDice to simulate throwing two 6-sided dice n times. On each throw, if the numbers on the two dice are equal, the score is twice the sum of the two throws. Otherwise the score is the sum of the two throws. Write statements to call the function once for each of two players, assigning the scores for 3 throws to `player1Score` and `player2Score`. [5]

```
function throwDice(n)[1]             //n is a parameter
    totalScore = 0[1]                //totalScore is a local variable
    //count is a local variable; its scope is the for...next loop
    for count = 1 to n[1]
        throw1 = random(1,6)         //throw1 is a local variable
        throw2 = random(1,6)[1]      //throw2 is a local variable
        score = throw1 + throw2[1]
        if (throw1 == throw2) then[1]
            score = 2 * score[1]
        endif
        totalScore = totalScore + score[1]
    next count
    return totalScore[1]
endfunction
player1Score = throwDice(3)
player2Score = throwDice(3)[1]
```

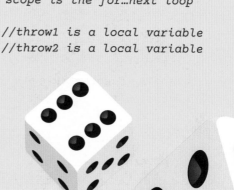

THE USE OF PROCEDURES

Procedures are similar to functions but are called simply by writing the name of the procedure, and any parameters in brackets. They do not return a value.

In Python, all subroutines have the same keyword `def()` to define a function or procedure.

Example:

```
procedure greet(firstName)
    print("Hello", firstName)
endprocedure
```

The procedure has one **parameter**, `firstName`. It is called by writing the procedure name, passing it the **argument** `"Joanna"` in brackets.

```
greet("Joanna")
```

This will print:

```
Hello Joanna
```

The example below defines a **global variable** called `logo` which can be used, changed or printed in the main program and in any of the procedures.

The procedure below displays a menu of options "1. Display rules", "2. Start new game", "3. Quit".

Complete the procedure and write a statement in the main program to call it. [3]

```
        global logo
        procedure menu()
            print(logo)
            print("1. Display rules")
            ........................
            etc.

    //main program
    logo = "C O U N T   T H E   C H I C K E N S"

    ........................  //call procedure

        global logo
        procedure menu()
            print(logo)
            print("1. Display rules")
            print("2. Start new game")[1]
            print("3. Quit")[1]
        endprocedure[1]

    //main program
    logo = "C O U N T   T H E   C H I C K E N S"
    menu()[1]
```

EXAMINATION PRACTICE

1. An organisation stores data about its employees.

    (a) State the most suitable data type for storing the following data:

       (i)   employee surname   [1]

       (ii) whether or not the employee has signed a contract of employment   [1]

       (iii) the number of days holiday they are entitled to per annum   [1]

       (iv) an employee's monthly salary   [1]

    (b) State the most appropriate data structure for storing all the personal data about employees.   [1]

    (c) Explain why this is the most suitable data structure.   [2]

2. Write a program which accepts a mark entered by the user, and prints it together with the word "Fail" if the mark is below 50, "Pass" if the mark is between 50 and 64, "Merit" if the mark is between 65 and 79, and "Distinction" if the mark is 80 or more.   [6]

3. The Boolean condition (`"a" in myName`) returns True if the string **myName** contains the character "a".

    (a) Write a Boolean condition that evaluates to True if the integer count does NOT contain the digit 7.   [3]

    (b) Write a program to print all the numbers between 1 and 100 except those that contain the digit 7 or those that are divisible by 5. E.g. 1, 2, 3, 4, 6, 8, 9, 11, 12...   [3]

4. A username is created by concatenating the first 2 letters of the user's first name, the first 3 letters of their surname (both converted to uppercase) and 6 digits giving their date of birth in the format ddmmyy.

    For example, Colin Brady, born 17/01/08 would have username COBRA170108.

    (a) What would be the username assigned to Mabel Green, born 29/02/2012?   [1]

    (b) Complete the program code snippet below to assign a username to Jayden Bullingden, born 12/05/2009.   [5]

    ```
    firstname = "Jayden"
    surname = "Bullingden"
    dob = "120509"
    ..............................
    ..............................
    etc.
    ```

5. (a) Describe the difference between a constant and a variable in a program.   [2]

    (b) Name **three** basic program structures and give an example of each.   [6]

6. (a) Write program code to define an array to hold the names of 6 children called: Anna, Dan, Peter, Sara, Vera, Zoe. Print the names of the 6 children on separate lines.   [3]

    (b) What type of search would you use to find out whether a particular name was in the array? Justify your answer.   [2]

7. A hockey team played six matches last year against each of five teams A, B, C, D and E.

The number of wins, draws and losses achieved in matches played against each team is recorded in a 2-dimensional array named **results** shown below.

	Wins	Draws	Losses
A	3	1	2
B	4	0	2
C	3	3	0
D	2	0	4
E	5	0	1

(a) The wins against team B are held in `results[1,0]`.

State the element of the array that holds the losses against Team D. [1]

(b) Write an algorithm to calculate and print the total number of draws scored overall. [4]

(You may assume the array **results** has already been defined with contents as shown.)

8. The function `triangle()` has 3 parameters a, b, c and returns **True** if $a^2 = b^2 + c^2$

(a) Use OCR ERL or a language of your choice to complete this function. [2]

```
function triangle(a, b, c)
    x = .....................
    y = .....................
    if x == y
        return True
    else
        return False
    endif
endfunction
```

(b) Code statements to pass three integers **sideA**, **sideB**, **sideC** to the function and print "**Right-angled**" if the function returns **True**, or "**Not right-angled**" if it returns **False**. [3]

9. A database table **Animal** is given below.

(a) Write an SQL query to return the **name**, **lifeSpanYears** and **animalClass** of all mammals with a lifespan of 5 years or more. [3]

animal	heartRateBPM	lifeSpanYears	animalClass	SpeedKmH
Blue Whale	8	90	Mammal	52
Giraffe	150	25	Mammal	60
Hamster	400	2	Mammal	6
Hummingbird	1200	5	Bird	79
Human	75	79	Mammal	45

(b) List the names of the animals which will be returned by the query. [1]

10. Explain what the following lines of code do:

```
nameFile = open("namefile.txt")
while not nameFile.endOfFile()
  memberRec = nameFile.readLine()
  print(memberRec)
endwhile
```
[4]

11. A parcel courier service uses a computer to calculate the cost of sending a parcel.

The program code is shown below:

```
01    global rate1, rate5, rate15
02    rate1 = 5.57
03    rate5 = 11.75
04    rate15 = 28.49
05    function parcelCost(weight)
06      overWeight = "Too heavy, parcel rates do not apply"
07      underWeight = "Send as package, not parcel"
08      if weight >= 20 then
09          theCost = overWeight
10      elseif weight >=15 then
11          theCost = str(rate15)
12      elseif weight >=5 then
13          theCost = str(rate5)
14      elseif weight >= 1 then
15          theCost = str(rate1)
16      else
17          theCost = underWeight
18      endif
19      return theCost
20    end function
21    //main program
22    parcelWeight = float(input("Enter parcel weight: "))
23    while parcelWeight != 0:
24      print("Postage cost: ", parcelCost(parcelWeight))
25      parcelWeight = float(input("Enter parcel weight: "))
26    endwhile
```

(a) Explain the purpose of line 01. [2]

(b) Give the line numbers of a section of code which is an example of iteration. [1]

(c) Give the line numbers of a section of code which is an example of selection. [1]

(d) Give **one** example of a local variable within the program. [1]

(e) Give **one** example of a parameter within the program. [1]

(f) At line 11, the function str() is used. State the purpose of this function. [1]

(g) The user inputs the following three parcel weights:

(i) 7.5
(ii) 0.7
(iii) 25

State what the output is in each case. [3]

DEFENSIVE DESIGN

Defensive design considerations

Anticipating misuse is an important stage of development. A programmer should never underestimate the level of creativeness, laziness or malice of users of a new system. Every possible input, however incorrect or creative should be anticipated. When validation or verification cannot resolve the issue, help messages and careful instruction should be used.

Authentication is a process used to test that a person is who they claim to be. Methods of authentication include a simple user ID and password, a PIN number or biometric methods such as fingerprint or facial recognition. These methods help to prevent unauthorised access to programs and data.

Input validation

Validation is the checking of data, on input, to ensure that it is sensible or reasonable. It cannot guarantee that the data is correct. Common methods include:

- **Range check:** a number or date is within an allowed range
- **Type check:** data is the right type such as an integer, character or text string
- **Length check:** text entered is not too long or too short – for example, a password is greater than 8 characters, a product description is no longer than 25 characters
- **Presence check:** checks that data has been entered, i.e. that a field has not been left blank
- **Format check:** checks that the format of, for example, a postcode or email address is appropriate

---

1. A tablet computer uses authentication to ensure that an authorised user is logging in.
   Describe **one** method of authentication. [3]

   Facial/fingerprint/voice recognition.[1] The user looks at a camera/touches a sensor/speaks into a microphone.[1] The computer scans the face/ fingerprint/analyses the voice pattern and compares it with previously captured and stored images/prints/recording analysis.[1] If they match, the user is authenticated.[1] A PIN or username and password can be entered. [1] If they match previously stored entries for that user[1], access is granted[1]. Pattern recognition asks a user to draw a pattern on the screen.[1] If this pattern matches a pattern pre-recorded by the user[1], access is permitted[1].

   Choose one method only in your answer and describe it for the remaining marks.

2. A date of birth field has been validated.

   (a) Explain how the validated date of birth field may still be incorrect.   [2]

   (b) Give **one** example of an invalid date of birth that should not be accepted.   [1]

   (a) A user may enter a date of birth of 10/05/2005[1], but their actual birthday was 19/05/2005.[1] This would be accepted by the computer as a valid date of birth.

   (b) Any year or date in the future[1], any day greater than 31 or less than 1[1], any month greater than 12 or less than 1[1]. E.g. 32/01/2005 or 31/02/2005.

Verification is the input of data twice. The two entries are compared and if they match, the entry is accepted as valid. Setting a new password commonly uses verification.

```
password = input("Please enter password: ")
passwordAgain = input("Confirm password: ")
if password == passwordAgain then
    print("Password accepted")
else
    print("Invalid - Passwords don't match")
endif
```

3. Describe **two** ways to ensure that personal data input to a database is accurate.   [4]

   Tip: *Select **two** answers from this list and give full descriptions of each.*

   Visual checks to spot obvious errors[1], input masks to limit entries in an incorrect format[1], dropdown boxes to restrict the possible entries[1], manual checking against an original source[1], verification to automatically check against another entry[1], printing data and checking against a hard copy[1], sending a copy of the recorded data to the person about whom the data relates so they can report any errors[1].

Maintainability

Decomposition of a problem involves breaking down a problem into its component parts.
Using **subprograms** (such as procedures and functions) helps to produce **structured code**.
Writing complex programs as a series of subprograms has many advantages:

- Makes debugging and maintaining the program easier as subprograms are usually no more than a page of code
- Subprograms can be tested separately and shown to be correct
- A particular subprogram can be called several times in the same program, and saved in a library to be used in other programs

Naming conventions help to identify variable names within code. Having a meaningful and consistent format for the naming of variables also helps readability. For example: `grandTotal` and `yearJoined`.
Indentation aids readability and in some programming languages is mandatory.

Commenting is used to document for yourself and others, the program name, the purpose of the program, complex areas of code and the purpose of each subprogram used. This helps ensure that the program can still be understood and maintained long after it was written. It should also indicate when and who wrote the program and who last updated it.

2.3.2

TESTING

The purpose of testing is to ensure that for any input, the program always works correctly. Your program may give correct results for some inputs, but does it work correctly for all possible inputs, including invalid ones?

Types of testing

Iterative testing is carried out using a pre-written test plan, finding and correcting errors in a program and retesting until all tests give the expected results. This is done during development. Each subprogram may be tested separately in a large program, as soon as it is written.

Final or **terminal testing** will be carried out when the program is completely finished and all parts of it have been separately tested. The user will test the program to check that all the required functions have been included, nothing is missing and everything works correctly whatever data is entered.

Syntax and logic errors

A **syntax error** will prevent your program from running. It is caused by a mistake in the spelling or 'grammar' of your code. For example `primt("Hello World")`. Syntax errors will be detected and reported by the compiler or interpreter.

A **logic error** is harder to spot. Your program will run but may give an incorrect or unexpected output. Common examples include the use of greater than or less than symbols, for example: using `x > 5` instead of `x >= 5` which could affect loop conditions or range checks, or missing brackets in mathematics calculations, for example:

    VAT = (orderTotal - discount) * taxRate gives a different answer to:

    VAT = orderTotal - discount * taxRate

Using a well thought-out test plan with the expected results manually calculated first should reveal any logic errors. Using a trace table may help to find and correct the errors.

Selecting and using suitable test data:

Test data should include:

- **normal data**, using examples of typical data that the program is designed to handle
- **boundary data** which includes both ends of an allowed range (e.g. 1–10) as well as data just outside this range (e.g. 0 or 11) that should not be allowed.
- **invalid data** which is data outside the limits of valid data
- **erroneous data**, for example non-numeric characters in a numeric field

Refining algorithms makes programs more efficient. For example, using a flag in a bubble sort to indicate when there have been no swaps in a single pass may reduce the execution time spent performing unnecessary passes after the list is already sorted.

EXAMINATION PRACTICE

1. An airline booking service permits up to four bags per passenger. A segment of code has been written to validate this input.

```
01  int(input("Enter number of bags: "))
02  if bagCount >= 0 OR bagCount <= 4 then
03      print("Bag allowance OK.")
04  else
05      print("Invalid bag allowance.")
06  endif
```

    (a) The program contains a logic error at line 02.

        (i) State what is meant by a logic error.   [1]

        (ii) Give an amended version of line 02 that corrects the error.   [1]

    (b) Identify **one** syntax error in the code.   [1]

    (c) Complete the test plan below to check that the valid range for bags is correct.   [5]

No.	Test purpose	Test data	Expected outcome
1	Check lowest valid number		Input is accepted
2	Check highest valid number		Input is accepted
3	Check invalid boundary data		Error message is displayed and user is asked to enter number again
4	Check valid entry		Input is accepted
5	Check erroneous entry		Error message is displayed and user is asked to enter number again

2. The statement below contains **two** syntax errors. Write the statements correctly.   [2]

```
int(input(mark))
if mark < 0 OR > 10 then
    print("Invalid mark entered")
endif
```

3. State the output of the following lines. Explain your answer.   [2]

```
total = int("175.82")
print("total")
```

4. Crackers is an online store. Data is being input to their customer database. The data includes a unique ID, surname, first name, three address fields, postcode, credit limit, date of last order.

    Name and briefly describe **four** types of validation check that may be used on the input data. [8]

5. Explain **three** ways in which a programmer can help to make a program as easy as possible to maintain. [6]

BOOLEAN LOGIC

The electronic circuits in a computer are constructed from **logic gates** which can only be in one of two states: on or off, 1 or 0. Three simple logic gates are shown below. Each is represented by a diagram and a truth table showing the possible outputs for each possible input.

AND gate (*Conjunction*)   **OR** gate (*Disjunction*)   **NOT** gate (*Negation*)

   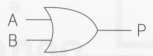   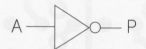

AND		
A	**B**	**P = A AND B**
0	0	0
0	1	0
1	0	0
1	1	1

OR		
A	**B**	**P = A OR B**
0	0	0
0	1	1
1	0	1
1	1	1

NOT	
A	**P = NOT A**
0	1
1	0

Logic gates can be combined to produce more complicated circuits. This circuit can be represented by the logic statement: P = (A AND B) OR (NOT B).

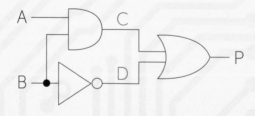

The truth table is given below.

A	B	C (A AND B)	D (NOT B)	P (C OR D)
0	0	0	1	1
0	1	0	0	0
1	0	0	1	1
1	1	1	0	1

1. Below is a logic diagram.

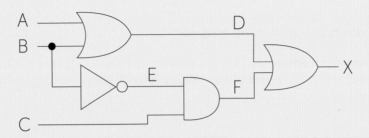

(a) Write the logic statements for D, E and F. [3]

(b) Write the logic statement corresponding to the logic diagram, in terms of inputs A, B and C and output X. Show your working. [4]

2. A logic circuit is being developed for a bus shelter advert that plays automatically if a passenger is detected in or around the bus stop.

- The system has two sensors, S1 and S2, that detect if a passenger is near. The advert plays if either of these sensors is activated.

- The advert should only play if it is not daytime (D).

- The output from the circuit, for whether the advert should play or not, is P.

(a) Write the logic statement for this system. [2]

(b) Complete the logic circuit for this system. [3]

1.   (a) D = A OR B[1], E = NOT B[1], F = C AND E[1]

      (b) X   = D OR F

               = (A OR B) OR (C AND E)

               = (A OR B)[1] OR[1] (C AND NOT B[1])[1]

2.   (a) P = (S1 OR S2)[1] AND (NOT D)[1]

      (b) [1 for each correct gate assuming the circuit is correct.]

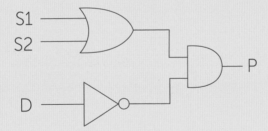

LANGUAGES

High- and low-level programming languages

A **high-level language** has a **syntax** and structure similar to English that is designed to be understood by humans. High-level code must be **compiled** or **interpreted** into machine code before it can be run.

```
speed = distance/time
print(speed)
```

Python, Visual Basic and Java are examples of high-level languages. These are hardware independent meaning they can be compiled for any system. The programmer can therefore concentrate on programming their algorithms rather than concerning themselves with the architecture of the computer. Assembly language is a **low-level language** which is used to control specific hardware components. The machine code produced by the assembler will occupy less space in memory, and will execute faster, than the machine code produced from a compiled program.

| Source code Written in a high-level language | Compiler | Object code (machine code) |

Translators

There are two main types of **translator**: a **compiler** and an **interpreter**. These work in different ways, each having different advantages.

Describe the need for a translator when using a high-level language. [2]

A translator (compiler or interpreter) converts high-level code into machine code or binary[1] to enable the code to be run[1].

Compiler	Interpreter
Translates the whole program in one go to produce object code	Translates and executes one line at a time
A compiled program executes faster as it is already in machine code	Takes more time to execute as each instruction is translated before it is executed
Produces an executable file so the original code does not need to be compiled again	Original code will be interpreted or translated every time it is run
No need for the compiler to be present when the object code is run	The interpreter must be installed to run the program

THE INTEGRATED DEVELOPMENT ENVIRONMENT (IDE)

An **IDE** is software used to enter and edit source code. It will also compile programs to machine code and have debugging features.

There are several tools or facilities of an IDE that are useful to programmers.

Error diagnostics (Debugging and error detection)

An **interpreter** or **compiler** highlights syntax errors in the code as you type or when you try to compile or run the code. Run-time errors will also be flagged up often giving the location of the error in the code and a description of the error.
Breakpoints can be set to pause a program at a certain point. This enables the programmer to check the value of variables at specific points in the code to find errors. A **watch window** is commonly used to display the value of specific variables as they change with each line of code. **Stepping** enables the programmer to step through line by line as they monitor changes in values.

Run-time environment

This enables a program to be run. Checks for run-time errors and other testing can be carried out.

Translator

The IDE will use either a **compiler** or **interpreter** to translate the high-level code into machine code so that it can be run.

Editor

The **editor** enables programmers to write and edit their code. **Syntax completion** functions often offer to complete code or suggest corrections. **Keywords** and different types of commands are commonly **highlighted** in different colours making the code easier to read. **Prettyprint** features enable code formatting, indentation and highlighting to be visible when printed.

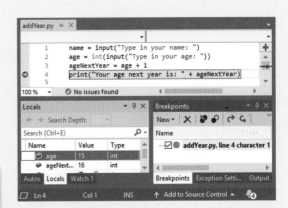

Explain what is meant by a run-time error.   [2]

A run-time error is one which will be detected when the program is run.[1] (E.g. a division by zero.[1]) It is not a syntax error, and may be caused by erroneous user input.[1]

EXAMINATION PRACTICE

1. Complete the truth table for P = A OR NOT B   [4]

A	B	NOT B	P
0			
0			

2. A motorbike has two tyres, front (F) and rear (R). If the ignition (I) is on, and either one of the tyres is below the minimum air pressure, a warning light is displayed.

    (a) Draw a logic circuit diagram for this scenario.   [2]

    (b) Complete the truth table for this scenario.   [5]

Front tyre pressure low (F)	Rear tyre pressure low (R)	Ignition on (I)	Working space (F or R)	Warning light on (W)
0	0	0		
0	0	1		

4. Shona is using a high-level language to learn programming.

    (a) Describe what is meant by a 'high-level language'.   [3]

    (b) Explain **two** features of an IDE (Integrated Development Environment) that can help
        Shona to find or prevent errors in her programming code.   [4]

5. (a) Explain the difference between a compiler and an interpreter.   [2]

    (b) PoundSoft is a software company selling accountancy software.

        The software is compiled rather than interpreted.
        Explain why they sell the software in this form.   [4]

EXAMINATION PRACTICE ANSWERS

1. D – Touch screen. [1]

2. B – A register in which the results of calculations are temporarily stored [1]

3. A – An area of internal HDD or SSD storage used when RAM is full. [1]

4. (a) Cache acts as a buffer between RAM and the CPU. Frequently requested data and instructions are transferred from RAM to cache. Cache is much faster than RAM so instructions and data can be accessed more quickly than from RAM. [3]
    (b) Cache is more expensive than RAM. [1]

5. For a computer's boot up instructions // to hold the program in an embedded device // to store the BIOS. [1]

6. (a) The control unit controls the input and output of data and the flow of data within the computer. It coordinates all the operations of the CPU, using clock timing signals to synchronise the stages of the Fetch-Decode-Execute cycle. [2]
    (b) The ALU carries out arithmetic operations such as adding two numbers, and logical operations such as AND, OR and NOT. [2]

7. One CPU may have more cache memory than the other which will speed up program execution as data and instructions can be retrieved much faster from cache. One CPU may have multiple cores, e.g. a dual-core computer will theoretically process twice as many instructions as a single core computer as the two cores can frequently process two instructions simultaneously. Disk access speed will affect the speed at which data is accessed and read from or written to storage e.g. SSD or HDD will affect this. A computer with more RAM will make less use of virtual memory, which slows down the execution of programs. Different architectures, for example PCs and Mac cannot be compared by clock speed alone as they perform differently at same clock speed. [4]
    (Tip: There are five points here – you only need two, but be sure to expand on each point you make. Just saying "One computer may have more cache" is not enough for two marks.)

8. SSD (or HDD). SSD is lightweight and unaffected by knocks or bumps as it has no moving parts. It runs with less power so increases the battery life of the tablet. It produces less heat when running so a fan is not required, saving space and weight inside the tablet. If HDD is chosen, they are fast, reliable and high capacity. An HDD may be less expensive to install making the overall tablet better value. [3]
    (Tip: Justification must match the answer you give. SSD is easier to justify here to gain 3 marks!)

1. (a) 4,500 bytes [1]   (b) 2,000 MB [1]   (c) (i) 00011100 [1]   (ii) Shifting one place right would divide the number by 2. [1]

2. (a) The set of characters or symbols that a computer can display using a particular representation, e.g. ASCII or Unicode. [1]
    (b) 160 bytes. [1]
    (c) (i) 1110, 1000. [2]
        (ii) Unicode uses more bytes (2 per character), which enables more characters/scripts to be represented. [2]

3. (a)

    (b) Lossy compression (JPG) would provide the smallest file size whilst maintaining a good quality image. Whilst some data is removed during the compression process, the image would still be recognisable. The smaller file size would mean it was able to download and display on a browser more quickly. Alternative compression methods such as PNG or GIF are acceptable with an explanation. [4]
    (c) Metadata is stored with the image data, to identify further information about the data, including its dimensions, bit depth, location data and file type. [2]

4. (a) Bit depth (or sample resolution) means the number of bits allocated to each recorded sample. [1]
    (b) The greater the number of bits, the more accurately the wave height of each sample can be recorded. This increases the overall quality of the recording as it will create a closer representation of the original sound. [2]
    (c) Sample rate is the number of samples taken each second. As the sample rate is increased, the file size will increase as each sample is saved at the given bit depth/resolution. [2]

1. (a) A protocol is a common set of rules used to transmit data. [1]
    (b) Without a set of rules which everything must follow, there would be no way to ensure that every browser could access every web server using the same methods. The World Wide Web would fail to operate. [2]
    (c) Web pages and other files, such as graphics, form part of the huge set of resources comprising the WWW. The WWW is one service on the Internet. The request and transmission of these resources from the web server to the client is done via the Internet. [2]
    (d) HTTP or HTTPS. [1]

2. (a) A Local Area Network is based over a small geographical area, using a company's or family's own cabling and network infrastructure. A Wide Area Network will commonly use third-party infrastructure to connect computers or networks that are distant from each other. [2]
    (b) (i) A router receives and transmits data within a network. It is used to join networks together, such as a connection to the Internet. It routes packets towards their destination. [1]
         (ii) A switch is used to connect multiple devices in a LAN together. It sends data between NICs using the MAC address of each device. [1]
    (c) A (web) host will in this case host the web pages, images and other files. The host will reply to requests for the web page, backup the files and keep the website online 24 hours a day. [2]

3. Bluetooth can create its own private ad-hoc network to connect devices within roughly 10m of each other. A Wi-Fi connection is unlikely to be available in many travel locations and would require setting up the speaker device and others on the Wi-Fi network with the permission of the network owner. A wired connection would remove the freedom of the user to move around with their mobile phone whilst remaining connected. [3]

4. (a) Encryption uses an algorithm and encryption key to encode data by the sender into ciphertext. The recipient computer uses their key to decode or decipher the text back into plaintext. [2]
    (b) Encrypting data by using protocols such as HTTPS prevents information from being understood if it is intercepted. This improves network security when transmitting confidential data, e.g. bank transactions or personal client data. [2]

5. (a) Cloud storage is the storage of files on remote servers, normally owned and maintained by a third-party organisation. [2]
    (b) Flexible storage capacity can be scaled up or down depending on requirements, so no need to purchase and maintain expensive storage devices which may be more than is currently required. The cloud storage provider is responsible for the security of data and regular backups, removing this responsibility from the organisation and reducing the requirement for computer maintenance staff. Cloud storage can be more environmentally friendly than millions of individual servers. [6]
    (c) You need a reliable connection to the Internet. Without a connection, you cannot access anything. Alternative answer: You have no direct control over the security of your data. Keeping your data on another company's server may cause issues of ownership and legal implications within the Data Protection Act (2018). You may be responsible for any security breaches over the data, even though you had no direct control over its security. [2]

6. (a) The browser first requests the IP address of the website from the DNS server. If the DNS server knows the IP address it sends it to the browser, if not, it requests it from a higher level DNS server and so on until it is found. The browser then sends the web page request to the website server at that IP address using an HTTP request. The website server performs any processing required for the web page and then sends back the web page and any images to the client using HTTP. The browser then renders the page on the screen for Su. [5]
    (b) Layers are self-contained so the technology in one layer can be redesigned or edited without affecting other layers. They break up a complex process into small, more manageable subdivisions. Layers enable different hardware and software designers to work on different layers. [2]

1. (a) A social engineering attack is an attempt to manipulate someone into giving away personal information such as bank account details or usernames and passwords so that they can access your computer. [2]
    (b) A 'phishing attack' is one way of performing a social engineering attack. An email or voice call will try to convince someone to give personal or confidential information or install a backdoor or keylogger to their computer.
        Social engineering attacks may involve phoning a receptionist in a company to gather information such as a name or days someone is on holiday or even a password. This can then be used for further attacks. [2]
    (c) A user should be aware of the signs of a typical phishing attack. and not click on links in an email from unknown sources or that have any suspicious content, or fall for emails which tell them their friend is in dire need of their financial help.
        Use spam filters, anti-virus software, and keep these up-to-date. [4]

2. (a) A DoS attack is when a server is deliberately flooded with thousands of fake requests within a short time period, usually from illegitimate IP addresses. This overwhelms the bandwidth and causes the system to crash. [2]
    (b) (i) The bank's customers will not be able to access their accounts. They may not be able to withdraw cash from ATMs or pay for anything using a debit card. [2]
         (ii) The bank may suffer a loss of reputation, leading to customers closing their accounts and moving their money. [2]

3. Sylvia could fall victim to a phishing attack and inadvertently allow a hacker access to her database. To reduce this risk she should learn how to recognise a possible phishing attack and never give access to a possible hacker.

   Her data may be hacked during transmission to and from clients. The firm should only use secure websites (https protocol) for which all transmissions are encrypted. Other risks such as malware, viruses, loss of data are also acceptable with a description. [4]

4. (a) Brute force attack: someone may attempt to guess Amy's password by trying (systematically or methodically) each possible password combination until the computer allows access. This is normally carried out by a computer program. [2]

   (b) Password security could be set up to limit the number of failed attempts before the device is locked. **Or**, her password could be made more secure by choosing a longer password containing upper and lower case characters, numbers and special characters which would increase the number of permutations. **Or**, penetration testing could highlight potential weaknesses so that they can be resolved through additional security. [3]

5. (a) The purpose of a firewall is to prevent unauthorised access to or from the school network. It monitors and controls incoming and outgoing traffic and controls what traffic is allowed to access or leave the network. All permitted traffic has to meet specified security criteria. Firewalls can be either hardware, software or a combination of both. [3]

   (b) Passwords should be a minimum of 8–10 characters and contain a mixture of uppercase, lowercase, numbers and special symbols. [2]

   (c) Have anti-virus software installed and make sure that this is kept up-to-date, by ensuring it is set to update automatically at least once a day. Keep operating systems up-to-date; an old operating system may have security weaknesses which allow hackers to gain entry. [2]

6. (a) The purpose of penetration testing is to detect weaknesses in an organisation's computer security systems, so that they can be fixed. [2]

   (b) A "white hat" hacker is employed to put themselves in the position of a dishonest employee to see if they can find a weakness in the security system and gain entry to parts of the system and data which they are not authorised to view or change. Any weakness is then reported, and extra security measures put in place to fix the vulnerability. [3]

Section 5

1. (a) Using multitasking, a computer switches rapidly between several jobs currently being processed, giving a small amount of processor time to each in turn. It therefore appears to the user(s) that all the jobs are being performed simultaneously. [3]

   (b) Memory management is provided by the operating system to manage programs and data that are stored in RAM. When a program is loaded memory management puts it into a free area of RAM. More programs or data can be loaded to different areas. This allows the operating system to multi-task and allow different programs to run in quick succession. When a program is closed it is removed from RAM. Memory management will also manage the use of virtual memory and the need to swap data in and out of RAM to a hard drive. [3]

2. Naming and saving files. Creating, renaming and deleting folders. Moving or copying files and folders between storage devices. Allocating user rights such as read-only, no access etc. to a folder or file. Searching for files, restoring deleted files. [4]

3. [5]

User interface	C
Memory management and multitasking	E
Peripheral management and drivers	A
User management	B
File management	D

4. (a) A disk becomes fragmented when there is limited available contiguous space left to save a file in one space. Instead, the file must be split into smaller fragments with each fragment stored in the smaller, remaining spaces on the disk. [1]

   (b) A defragmentation utility can help by moving all of the files around on the disk, putting each fragmented file back together again so that each file is stored in consecutive blocks. This makes searching for the file much faster as the computer needs only to move to one section of the hard disk rather than thrashing to many different locations. Saving a file is similar in that the computer can place a whole file in one area on the disk rather than lots of smaller fragments in different locations. [2]

5. (a) Smartphone = GUI, ATM = menu driven. [2]

   (b) A GUI is a much more flexible and powerful interface, enabling many tasks to be performed with a single mouse click or touch. Multiple windows that enable you to copy data between applications by dragging and dropping. Icons make it more intuitive to see what functions are used for. Pop-up menus appear on right-clicking the mouse, and the pointer or mouse cursor makes it easy to navigate around the screen. [2]

6. Encryption uses an algorithm to encode data into another form which can only be decoded and interpreted by someone with the correct encryption key. [3]

Section 6

1. The volume of e-waste is increased. Working equipment is sometimes unnecessarily sent to landfill in the UK, and also sent abroad to be disposed of. This is a waste of resources, especially rare raw materials used in the latest technology that must be mined to be replaced. Mining causes significant environmental damage and some metals are already running short in supply. Toxic chemicals used in the manufacture of hardware can leak into the environment if left in landfill. Some nations receive our e-waste and extract valuable metals through burning equipment which pollutes the air, waterways and the land. [6]

2. (a) The copyright to the code will be owned by the programmer or company. If they have allowed it to be copied then James can legally do this. They may have created other restrictions, such as the need to acknowledge the original programmer or release the new adaptation and source code for free. If James doesn't act within the terms of the licence then he would be breaking the Copyright, Designs and Patents Act. It would be ethical to develop using someone else's code if within the terms of the licence. If outside the terms, it would be unethical as it deprives the original creator of their work and possibly income. [4]

   (b) Proprietary: Users have no access to the source code so cannot modify the program.

   Open source: Users do have access to the source code and can modify it. They will usually need to provide details of their changes to others who want the source code. [4]

   (c) Open source software is likely to be used by more people. This can help boost James' reputation and could help him generate income through advertising. Having more users means a greater pool of contributors which can result in faster development of the software. [2]

3. [5]

Action	The Data Protection Act 2018	Computer Misuse Act 1990	Copyright Designs and Patents Act 1988
Unlicensed image			X
Collecting and selling customer details	X		
Guessing someone's smartphone PIN		X	
Failure to change inaccurate customer details	X		
Unauthorised access and modification of accounts		X	

Section 7

1. (a) 13 (the number of items in the list) [1]
   (b) 3 6 7 [3]
   (c) 9 found at position 3 (item 9 is the 4th in the list, counting from 0) [1]
   (d) It performs a linear search on the list for an item entered by the user. If the item is not found, it prints "Invalid number"). [2]

2. (a) It acts as a 'flag' which is set to False when a pass through the list is made and no items are swapped, meaning that the list is now sorted. [2]
   (b) ```
temp = names[index]
names[index] = names[index+1]
names[index+1] = temp
``` [3]
   (c) Adam Edna Charlie Jack Ken Maria Victor
       Adam Charlie Edna Jack Ken Maria Victor [2]
   (d) 3 passes. Swaps are made on the first two passes. The list will be sorted after the second pass, and on the third pass, no swaps are made, so swapMade is set to False and the while loop terminates. [2]

3. (a) Algorithmic thinking [1]
   (b) Decomposition [1]
   (c) Abstraction [1]

4. (a) [4]

| num | a | b | ans |
|---|---|---|---|
| | 0 | 0 | 0 |
| 3 | 3 | 1 | 0 |
| 8 | 11 | 2 | 0 |
| 2 | 13 | 3 | 0 |
| 5 | 18 | 4 | 0 |
| -1 | | | 4.5 |

   (b) It calculates the average of the numbers input by the user. [1]
```

Section 8

1. (a) (i) string   (ii) Boolean   (iii) integer   (iv) real/float   [4]
   (b) File of records/database.   [1]
   (c) It is easy to search a database for a record, satisfying given criteria using SQL.   [2]

2.
```
mark = input("Please enter mark: ")
if mark >= 80 then
    print(mark, " Distinction")
elseif mark >= 65 then
    print(mark, "Merit")
elseif mark >= 50 then
    print(mark, "Pass")
else
    print(mark, "Fail")
endif            (Tip: First test for mark >=80. A mark >= 80 is also >= 50.)
```
[6]

   Alternative answer:
```
mark = input("Please enter mark: ")
if mark < 50 then
    print(mark, "Fail")
elseif mark <=64 then
    print(mark, "Pass")
elseif mark <= 79 then
    print(mark, "Merit")
else
    print(mark, "Distinction")
endif
```
[6]

3. (a) `NOT("7" in str(count))` (*Tip: You should convert the integer 7 and the integer count to strings.*)   [3]
   (b)
```
for count = 1 to 100
    if NOT ("7" in str(count)) AND NOT (count MOD 5 == 0) then
        print(count)
    next count
```
[3]

4. (a) MAGRE290212   [1]
   (b)
```
ucaseFirstname = firstname.upper
ucaseSurname = surname.upper
username = ucaseFirstname.left(2) + ucaseSurname.left(3) + dob
```
[5]

5. (a) The value of a constant cannot change during program execution. The value stored in a variable can be changed.   [2]
   (*Tip: Remember, it is the **value** of a variable, not the variable itself, which can be changed.*)
   (b) Sequence:
```
      a = 1
      b = 2
      c = a + b
```
   Selection:
```
      if a == b then
          print("a and b are equal")
      endif
```
   Iteration:
```
      for count = 1 to 10
          print(2^count)
      next count
```
[6]

6. (a)
```
array name[6]
name = ['Anna', 'Dan', 'Peter', 'Sara', 'Vera', 'Zoe']
for n = 0 to 5
  print(name[n])
next n
```
[3]
   (*Tip: remember that the first element of the array is name[0]*)
   (b) A linear search because there are only 6 names and it is much simpler to code than a binary search.   [2]

7. (a) `results[3,2]`   [1]
   (b)
```
totalDraws = 0
for row = 0 to 4
  totalDraws = totalDraws + results[row, 1]
next row
print(totalDraws)
```
[4]

8. (a) `x = a*a`   (or alternatively, `x = a^2`)
    `y = b*b + c*c`   (or alternatively, `x = b^2 + c^2`) [2]

  (b)
```
if triangle(sideA, sideB, sideC) then
    print("Right-angled")
else
    print("Not right-angled")
endif
```
  [3]

  (*Tip:* you could alternatively write something like the following)
```
RtAngle = triangle(sideA, sideB, sideC)
if RtAngle == True then …
```

9. (a) SELECT name, lifeSpanYears, animalClass
    FROM Animal
    WHERE animalClass = 'mammal' AND lifeSpanYears >= 5 [3]

  (b) Blue Whale, Giraffe, Human [1]

10. Opens a text file saved as **namefile.txt**. Assigns the open file to the variable **nameFile**. Reads and prints every record in the file. [4]

11. (a) It declares three variables as global. Global variables are recognised, and their values can be changed, anywhere in the program including subroutines. [2]

  (b) Lines 23-26 [1]

  (c) Lines 08-18 [1]

  (d) overWeight, underWeight, theCost [1]

  (e) weight [1]

  (f) It converts the floating point value 28.49 to a string, "28.49" [1]

  (g) (i) Postage cost: 11.75
      (ii) Postage cost: Send as package, not parcel
      (iii) Postage cost: Too heavy, parcel rates do not apply [3]

Section 9

1. (a) (i) A logic error will not prevent the program from running but will produce an unexpected or erroneous output. [1]
      (ii) `if bagCount >= 0 AND bagCount <=4 then` [1]

  (b) There are two syntax errors in line 01. **bagCount** needs to be initialised and the input needs to be converted into an integer. Correcting both errors, line 01 should be written: **bagCount = int(input("Enter number of bags: "))** [1]

  (c) [5]

No.	Test purpose	Test data	Expected outcome
1	Check lowest valid number	0	Input is accepted
2	Check highest valid number	4	Input is accepted
3	Check invalid boundary data	-1, 5	Error message is displayed and user is asked to enter number again.
4	Check valid entry	2	Input is accepted
5	Check erroneous entry	!(Any non-numeric character)	Error message is displayed and user is asked to enter number again.

2. `mark = int(input("Enter mark "))`
   `if mark < 0 OR mark > 10 then…` [2]

3. **total** (because the word "total" in quotes is a string, not a variable name). [2]

4. ID – presence check, format check, length check if all IDs are of a specific length and format.
   Postcode – format check to ensure it is in a correct format.
   credit limit – range check to ensure that it is within a specified range, presence check to ensure that an amount has been entered, type check, must be real/float/currency.
   date of last order – correct date format e.g. dd/mm/yyyy, range check, e.g. must be less than current date. [8]

5. Comments in the program to say what the program does, who wrote it and when, how tricky parts of the program work.
   Make use of short subprograms / functions / procedures which can be modified and tested separately.
   Use a standard e.g. camelCase for variable names.
   Use indentation to show where loops or selection statements begin and end.
   Use uppercase / snake case for constants to make them easier to differentiate from variables. [6]

1.

[4]

A	B	NOT B	P
0	0	1	1
0	1	0	0
1	0	1	1
1	1	0	1

2. (a)

[5]

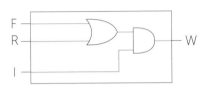

(b)

[2]

Front tyre pressure low (F)	Rear tyre pressure low (R)	Ignition on (I)	D = F OR R	Warning light on (W)
0	0	0	0	0
0	0	1	0	0
0	1	0	1	0
0	1	1	1	1
1	0	0	1	0
1	0	1	1	1
1	1	0	1	0
1	1	1	1	1

3. (a) D = A OR B, E = NOT B, F = C AND E [3]

(b) X = D OR F

= (A OR B) OR (C AND E)

= (A OR B) OR (C AND NOT B) [4]

4. (a) A high-level language is written in an English-like syntax. It is not particular to any type of hardware so can be compiled or translated for use on other systems. High-level code must be translated into machine code before it can be executed. [3]

(b) A text editor can highlight syntax errors in the code and make suggestions for auto-completing some lines of code. Autoindentation can to help make the code easier to read and diagnose errors. (Some languages prevent indentation errors.) Breakpoints and stepping allow the programmer to run the program line by line. Variables can be watched to check when and how their values change. [4]

5. (a) A compiler translates the whole program, producing object code which may be saved and run without the need to recompile. An interpreter translates and runs each line of code one by one. [2]

(b) PoundSoft sells the software in compiled form (object code) so that the purchaser does not need to have an appropriate interpreter installed on each of their computers. The compiled code is executable, unlike code which has to be interpreted every time before it can be run.

A second reason is that if they do not sell the source code, no one can copy and/or amend it, and possibly resell a similar package. This also protects any clever algorithms they may have developed as no one can see how they work. [4]

BAND DESCRIPTIONS AND LEVELS OF RESPONSE GUIDANCE FOR EXTENDED RESPONSE QUESTIONS

Questions that require extended writing use mark bands. The whole answer will be marked together to determine which mark band it fits into and which mark should be awarded within the mark band.

Mark Band 3 — High Level (6–8 marks)

- Technical terms have been used precisely
- The answer is logical and shows an extensive understanding of Computer Science concepts, and principles
- The answer is almost always detailed and accurate
- All parts of the answer are consistent with each other
- Knowledge and ideas are applied to the context in the question
- Where examples are used, they help with understanding the answer
- Arguments and points are developed throughout the answer with a range of different perspectives. Different sides of a discussion are considered against each other

Mark Band 2 — Mid Level (3–5 marks)

- The meaning of technical terms in the question has been understood
- The answer shows an understanding of Computer Science concepts
- Arguments and points are developed in the answer, but sometimes useful examples or related knowledge to the context have not been included
- Some structure has been given to the answer with at least one line of reasoning
- Sound knowledge has been effectively shown

Mark Band 1 — Low Level (1–2 marks)

- The answer shows that technical terms used in the question have not been understood
- Key Computer science concepts have not been understood and have not been related to the context of the question
- The answer is only loosely related to the question and some inaccuracies are present
- Gaps are shown in Computer Science knowledge
- The answer only considers a narrow viewpoint or one angle
- The answer is unstructured
- Examples used are mostly irrelevant to the question or have no evidence to support them

0 marks

- No answer has been given or the answer given is not worth any marks

The above descriptors have been written in simple language to give an indication of the expectations of each mark band. See the OCR website at **www.ocr.org.uk** for the official mark schemes used.

INDEX

Symbols

2D array 69

A

abstraction 47, 49
accumulator 3
algorithmic thinking 47
algorithms
  compression 21
  encryption 30
  identifying 58
  searching 54
  sorting 55
ALU 3
amplitude 20
analogue sound 20
anticipating misuse 78
anti-malware software 35
architecture of the CPU 2
Arithmetic Logic Unit 2
arithmetic operators 62
arrays 68
ASC() 67
ASCII 17
assignment 61
authentication 78

B

bandwidth 23
binary 11
  addition 13
  counting 12
  representation of images 18
  search 54, 58
  shifts 16
  to denary 12
  to hexadecimal 14
bit 11
bit depth 18, 20
bitmap 18, 21
blagging 34
Bluetooth 29
bool() 66
Boolean
  conditions 62
  data type 66
  logic 82

boundary data 80
breakpoint 85
brute-force attack 34
bubble sort 51, 55, 58
byte 11

C

cabling 29
cache 3, 4
Caesar cipher 30
camelCase 61
capacity 9, 11
case statement 63
casting 66
CD 8
characters 17
character set 17
CHR() 67
ciphertext 30
client-server network 26
clock speed 2, 4
Cloud 28
coaxial cable 29
colour depth 18
commenting 79
common errors 53
comparison operators 62
compiler 84
compression
  lossy / lossless 21
  software 38
computational thinking 47
Computer Misuse Act 1990 43
concatenation 67
condition-controlled loop 65
constants 61
Control Unit 2
copper coaxial cable 23
Copyright Designs and Patents
     Act 43
cores 2, 5
cost 9
count-controlled loop 64
CPU
  clock 2
  instruction 2
  performance 4
cultural issues 40

D

database 70
data compression software 38
Data Protection Act 2018 43
data storage 11
data types 66
debugging 79, 85
decomposition 47, 49
defensive design 78
defragmentation software 38
denary
  to binary 12
  to hexadecimal 15
denial of service attack 34
dentifying inputs 48
DIV 62
Domain Name Server 28
drivers 37
dual-coding iii
durability 9

E

editors 85
embedded system 4
encryption 30, 35, 38
environmental issues 40
erroneous data 80
error
  detection 85
  diagnostics 85
  overflow 13
Ethernet 29
ethical issues 40

F

fetch-execute cycle 2, 4
fibre optic cable 23, 29
field 70
file handling operations 72
file management 37
file server 26
file size 19
firewall 35
float() 66
flowcharts 50
format check 78
forms of attack 34

EXAMINATION TIPS

With your examination practice, use a boundary approximation using the following table. Be aware that boundaries are usually a few percentage points either side of this.

Grade	9	8	7	6	5	4	3	2	1
Boundary	90%	80%	70%	60%	50%	40%	30%	20%	10%

1. Be aware of command words at the back of the specification. If 'describe' or 'explain' questions are given you need to expand your answers. To help you justify your responses, aim to include words such as BECAUSE... or SO... in every answer because this forces you to justify your point, so you get additional marks. See how well it works!

2. Explain questions such as 'explain why this is the most appropriate...' do not require just a list of benefits. Instead you should identify the benefits and then expand each one, applying them to the scenario or context.

3. Full answers should be given to questions – not just key words. Make your answers match the context of the question.

4. Algorithm questions require an actual algorithm not a repetition of the question.

5. If a question explicitly asks for an algorithm to be written in pseudocode, then it will not gain marks if it is written as a flowchart. Equally, a question that asks for an algorithm to be written as a flowchart will not gain marks if answered with pseudocode.

6. If you have difficulties with algorithm questions, remember that you will gain marks (where appropriate) for input and output statements.

7. The statement `INPUT = variableName` will not gain marks in pseudocode as the variable name needs to be on the left of the assignment operator. E.g. `variableName = INPUT`.
    `INPUT variableName` is an acceptable alternative.

8. String concatenation is not enough for an output e.g. `print(hello + name)` – the string must be in quotes, e.g. `print("hello " + name)`

9. Generic answers are not sufficient. E.g. If a question asks for a description of the function of a router, an answer 'it connects devices together' is not sufficient. Instead answers should describe how routers are used to receive packets from computers, read the destination address of each and then forward each packet to its destination. Faster, bigger and cheaper are not very useful responses unless you justify your point.

10. The pseudocode you write does not need to match any precise syntax as long as it can "be reasonably inferred by a competent programmer".

11. Arrays will always start at zero, not 1.

12. Remember that a nested loop completes fully for each iteration of the outer loop.

13. In pseudocode, `input("enter name")` will not gain marks as the result needs to be assigned to a variable to store it – e.g. `name = input("enter name")`. Equally, two values cannot be input at the same time as a variable will only store one value. Instead, use `a = INPUT("Enter a")` then `b = INPUT("Enter b")`.
    `INPUT a, b` would be an acceptable alternative.

14. A common error in IF statements is `if name != "Sam" or "sam" then`.
    This should be: `if name != "Sam" or name != "sam" then`

15. Be careful with quotes around strings. E.g. `choice = A` (which assigns a variable) is very different to `choice = "A"` (which assigns a string).

    Good luck!